INTERNATIONAL PRIESTS IN AMERICA

International Priests in America

Challenges and Opportunities

Dean R. Hoge
and
Aniedi Okure, O.P.

LITURGICAL PRESS
Collegeville, Minnesota

www.litpress.org

| 06 | 07 | 08 | 09 | 10 | 5 | 4 | 3 | 2 | 1 |

Library of Congress Cataloging-in-Publication Data

Hoge, Dean R., 1937–
    International priests in America : challenges and opportunities / Dean R. Hoge and Aniedi Okure.
        p.   cm.
    Includes bibliographical references and index.
    ISBN-13: 978-0-8146-1830-1 (pbk. : alk. paper)
    ISBN-10: 0-8146-1830-8 (pbk. : alk. paper)
    1. Catholic Church—United States—Clergy—History—20th century. 2. Immigrants—United States—History—20th century. I. Okure, Aniedi. II. Title.

BX1407.C6H62 2006
262'.14273—dc22

2005029797

Contents

Foreword

In 1965 the United States changed the immigration law that allowed for people from Asia and Latin America to enter the United States in unprecedented numbers. The two coasts experienced an explosion of new immigrants. The immigrants' social and institutions have been working hard to meet the needs of these new communities ever since. Over the years the new wave of immigrants has reached even into the heartland.

The church knows the struggles of these new immigrants. It has played a major role in helping them to settle in this country, much in the same way that it helped the European immigrants in the late eighteenth and early nineteenth centuries.

What the church was not prepared for was the phenomenon of fewer clergy here in the United States, challenging its ability to minister to well-established Catholic communities as well as to the new immigrant population. The traditional clergy of the United States have found themselves scrambling to meet the needs of the diverse faith communities.

Gradually the church has seen growing numbers of new immigrant clergy taking positions in Catholic churches across the United States as pastors, associates, and extern clergy. Questions have arisen about the nature of this phenomenon. Are priests born in other countries here to serve their own immigrant people, as was the pattern of the European immigrant clergy? Are they here to evangelize and be on mission to an American population in need of a new evangelization? Have they come in response to fewer priestly vocations in the United States? What is their effectiveness? How are they received? Is this a pastoral solution to the problem of fewer priests? These and many other questions have arisen with the growing numbers of foreign-born priests beginning to serve the Catholic population of the United States.

For many years this situation has caused concern for the National Federation of Priests' Councils. In the fall of 2000 the federation sponsored a symposium that sought to consider the reality of international priests and to surface issues and questions that were swirling around it. The study and its commentaries presented in this book were occasioned by that symposium.

The National Federation of Priests' Councils is pleased to present this study for the consideration of the Catholic community as it seeks to understand itself in the new reality of a globally oriented church in the United States. We are extremely grateful to Dr. Dean Hoge and Father Aniedi Okure for their tireless efforts on behalf of this project. It is sure to be a major contribution to the pastoral life of the Catholic Church in the United States at the beginning of this third millennium.

Rev. Robert J. Silva
President, The National Federation of Priests' Councils

Preface

As the Catholic Church in America brings in more and more international priests to serve in the United States, debate is spreading about if and how this should be done. Criticisms, proposals, and suggestions are being heard on all sides of the issues, and they commonly call for more research and information.

The National Federation of Priests' Councils, in responding to these voices, held symposia in 2001 and 2002 on international priests in America. As a result, it decided to commission new research and suggested that the first project should be a depiction of the existing situation and the attitudes of priests and laity today. It preferred to limit attention to the international priests whose ministry in the United States began in 1985 or later. The 1985 cutoff meant that new research would look solely at the most recent arrivals rather than reviewing the earlier international priests, largely Irish, who arrived in the forties, fifties, and sixties.

Accordingly, the target group to be studied was defined as all priests born overseas (including Puerto Rico) whose ministry in the United States began in 1985 or later. Priests who are students, educators, or administrators are included if they engage in sacramental ministry. Dean Hoge was asked to begin the research process.

Work began in 2002 with pilot studies to see if a reliable list of international priests could be compiled and if everyone involved—foreign-born priests, American priests, vicars, personnel boards, and lay ministers—would cooperate with the surveys and interviews we would need. Father Aniedi Okure was then added to the project.

This book is our report. We have spent two years surveying dioceses and religious institutes about their policies, then surveying a sample of international priests about their experiences and recommendations. In the past year we have talked with a hundred key persons personally and by phone; eighty-seven of the interviews were taped and transcribed. We also held three focus groups. The process is described in the Appendix.

As soon as we started, we discovered that we were in the middle of a swirling discussion on several levels. Our interviews led to broad-ranging questions about ministry, vocations, missions, and finances. We were not in any position to take stands on ecclesiological questions; we defined our task as social science analysis, not theological judgment. Our job was to gather data and listen to recommendations from all sides, then to convey them in print.

This book, therefore, states the issues as clearly and fairly as possible without attempting to settle them. If the reader feels a lack of closure in what we offer here, it is because today there is a lack of closure in the church. We left it to the four commentators at the end of the book, persons selected as wise and capable voices of the church, to spell out the implications of the findings.

We co-authors brought years of experience to this project. Dean Hoge has carried out (in collaboration with others) five surveys of American priests in the last two decades; the results have been published in articles and books, mainly *The Future of Catholic Leadership: Responses to the Priest Shortage* (1987), *The First Five Years of the Priesthood* (2002), and *Evolving Visions of the Priesthood* (2003). Father Aniedi Okure, O.P., served as coordinator of ethnic ministries at the United States Catholic Conference from 1995 to 2001, during which time his main task was gathering information and opinions about international priests and religious, organizing orientation workshops, and serving as staff writer for the book *Guidelines for Receiving Pastoral Ministers in the United States*. We have formed our own opinions about the various issues, but for the most part we have kept our views to ourselves. Only in the final chapter do we state a few of our conclusions.

From the beginning we saw that we were dealing basically with two issues. First, should the Catholic Church in the United States bring in more international priests in future years? Second, with the assumption that for better or worse some will be brought in, how should this be done in a way that furthers the ministry of the priests and advances the mission of the church? We have structured the book to address these two issues. The first part of the book is on the debate about *if* we should bring in more foreign-born priests, and the second part is on *how* this should be done.

The first chapter introduces the present-day situation by reviewing the history of international priests in the United States. Chapter 2 describes the international priests serving in the United States in 2004. Chapter 3 analyzes the global brain drain and the worldwide distribution of priests. Chapters 4 and 5 set forth arguments about whether America should continue to bring in international priests. Chapter 6 continues the topic by looking more precisely at the motivations of international priests who come here.

Chapter 7 is devoted to conveying the feelings of international priests in our interviews and focus groups. Chapter 8 takes up questions of screening candidates, language training, cultural sensitivity, and finances. Chapter 9 presents information on programs of acculturation now being offered by dioceses and religious institutes. Chapter 10 states a few conclusions and reports the recommendations we gathered from the international priests, American priests, vicars, and lay leaders.

We asked four leaders of the American Catholic Church to read the first draft of our report and write commentaries from their points of view.

D. H. and A. O.

Acknowledgments

This project could not have been completed without the help of many persons. From the beginning we were encouraged by the national leaders of the National Federation of Priests' Councils, especially the president, Bob Silva, and two administrators, first Bernard Stratman and later Vic Doucette. We had two meetings of an advisory committee, which included Robert Silva, Vic Doucette, Cletus Kiley, Anthony McGuire, and Eugene Hemrick. Allan Deck, Kenneth McGuire, Eduardo Fernandez, Kathryn Pierce, John Kemper, Anthony Dao, Bernard Stratman, and Boguslaw Augustyn that gave us extensive help and advice. Our surveys of dioceses, institutes, and international priests were carried out with the extensive help of Florencio Riguera. Florencio also carried out most of the data handling. We were assisted in interviewing by Eugene Hemrick, and transcribing was done by Lele Yang, Xiaofan Li, Florence Cole, and Claudia Penn. Library assistance was offered by Hannah Simon and Merlyn Kettering. Other research assistants were Jacqueline Wenger and Tom Norton. Financial support was provided by a grant from the Louisville Institute for the Study of American Religion and from an anonymous donor. We thank all these people.

The project was commissioned by the National Federation of Priests' Councils, but they are not responsible for the outcome; we authors bear that responsibility. We pray that the project will help the church carry out its God-given mission.

Chapter 1

International Priests in American History

The Catholic Church in the United States has always had international priests serving its parishes, and in most of its history it depended on them. Only in one short period, from about 1940 to 1960, did Americans produce enough homegrown priests. The rest of the time foreign priests were present in great numbers, and at times dominated the church.

In the pre-revolutionary period Catholics were few in number in the colonies, and there were few priests. Religious priests dominated, mainly Jesuits. In the 1780s, after the Revolutionary War, there were only twenty-one priests in the entire nation—nineteen in Maryland and two in Pennsylvania (Perko 1989, 99). In 1791 French Sulpicians, a society of diocesan priests, began arriving, and they had a major influence. They worked in parishes and in missions, and they established the first seminary in the new nation, St. Mary's in Baltimore (Perko 1989, 107–08).

The early Catholic communities in the United States produced very few native-born priests. In 1791, at the first church synod, held in Baltimore, 80 percent of the clergy present were foreign-born. French priests were the most common, and for the most part, the French priests were refugees seeking asylum during the French Revolution. These men, and indeed most of the European priests, tended to be suspicious of republican tendencies in America and preferred to reproduce the European church here (Dolan 1985, 118–20).

The American bishops needed to look to Europe for priests, and they did so at every opportunity. They wrote their friends and confreres in Europe and sent recruiters to European seminaries to try to attract new priests to come to the United States. They met with some success, since French and Irish seminaries had a surplus of graduates. For instance, in 1835, Simon Brute, the first bishop of St. Louis, traveled to France, and in 1836 he returned with eleven priests, two deacons, two subdeacons, three men in minor orders, and two other ecclesiastical students (Ellis 1971, 17).

Not all of the immigrant priests in those earlier years were ministerial successes. Many were inspiring contributors to church growth, but others were simply troublemakers (Hennessy 1981, 91). The letters of early American bishops are filled with complaints about the priests from Europe. There were mainly two complaints. First, as already mentioned, the European priests preferred a more hierarchical, less republican-style church than the Americans did, and they could not understand the American separation of church and state.

Second, many of the foreign-born priests were unable to get along with their religious superior or bishop. Some were "freelance" clerics who came to America on their own. The American bishops complained to their European colleagues that due to the shortage, they were forced to accept almost any priest, but they found out that many priests who came here were misfits and malcontents back in their home countries. The archbishop of Baltimore, in an 1819 letter to the Holy See, stated that out of the ten Irish priests who came to his diocese, eight had turned out badly (Gannon 1971, 304). European bishops sometimes viewed America as a kind of a dumping ground for wayward priests. This tendency, as we might expect, did not endear them to the bishops in America (Morris 1997, 129).

In the Southwest the problem of the shortage of priests was the same as in the East. A few priests came in from Mexico, but many more were needed, and French priests were invited. This solved one problem but produced another: tensions arose between the fairly relaxed Hispanic Catholic laity and the more religiously rigorous French clergy (Perko 1989, 194).

Regardless of these problems, a great many foreign priests became bishops in the United States. At the second plenary council, held at Baltimore in 1866, thirty of the forty-seven bishops present were foreign-born (Hennessey 1981, 160). Dolan describes the dominance of foreign-born priests in the nineteenth century:

> Throughout the nineteenth century, the vast majority of these [priest] recruits were foreign-born; the few studies of the clergy that have been done illustrate this very clearly. In Minnesota, for example, nine out of ten priests, between 1844 and 1880, were foreigners; in the next thirty years the ratio dropped off to two out of three, but this was still a very high percentage. . . . In St. Louis a similar pattern prevailed at the turn of the century, with over half of the clergy being immigrants. Reflecting the nationality of the people, the vast majority of these priests, at least 70 percent in Minnesota, were Irish and Germans. (1992, 170)

Whereas priests came from various European nations, including France, Germany, and Italy, the vast majority came from Ireland.

The Coming of the Irish

The large Irish immigration beginning in the 1830s brought with it a wave of Irish priests. Ireland in the nineteenth century had an abundance of priests, and the bishops directed thousands of seminary graduates to go into mission work—above all, in the United States, but also in Canada, England, Scotland, and Australia. By the end of the nineteenth century, Irish priests were the most common foreign-born priests in the United States. About four thousand came between 1840 and today. Most were diocesan, not religious, priests and most served in the South and the West. Americans dubbed them the "F.B.I."—the "Foreign-Born Irish." Florida and California had large concentrations. William Smith cites statistics:

> By the mid-1800s, 59 percent of the priests in the diocese of New York were Irish-born and at the beginning of the twentieth century, 62 percent of the bishops were Irish-American, more than half of them being Irish-born. By 1900 two-thirds of the diocesan priests in the diocese of St. Paul, Minnesota, were foreign-born with more than one-quarter of them being Irish. One-third of the pastors in the Archdiocese of San Francisco in 1963 were born and educated in Ireland, while during the 1940s and 1950s, 80 percent of the priests in the Archdiocese of Los Angeles were Irish-born. (2004, 14)

Irish priests were readily available, since the seminaries produced more than could be placed, and the bishops in Ireland simply assigned many young men to minister overseas. Not all who went to other nations liked ministering there, and some returned to Ireland as quickly as they could. Others grew fond of their adopted land and stayed their entire lives. America, especially, offered more opportunities and more possibilities of parish growth. Also, priests in America were promoted to become pastors much more quickly than in Ireland. American bishops were appreciative, but there are some indications in their papers that they suspected they were not getting the best from the Irish seminaries (Smith 2004, 22).

Wherever the Irish priests served, they were directed to serve all ethnic groups, and soon they were presiding over parishes of Bohemians, Slovaks, Italians, and Portuguese. They acquired a reputation of being more rigorous and disciplined than priests from Italy, Spain, or Portugal. The laity from these nations preferred their own priests whenever they could find one (Morris 1997, 129).

Monsignor William Barry, an Irish priest in south Florida in the 1920s, 1930s, and 1940s, was an example of how Irish priests helped one another.

> For over thirty years he held a card game for Irish priests on Sunday evenings. It has been noted that some clergy believed the Irish priests were clannish and that this hindered ties with native-born clergy. If the Irish priests

were indeed clannish this is just one example of maintaining a subcultural identity. Sharing activities on free days, annual visits to Ireland, and annual seminary reunions held in the United States were other means by which these priests reinforced their Irish identity. (Smith 2004, 69)

Smith's Survey of Irish Priests

William Smith in 1997 carried out an important survey of Irish-born and Irish-educated diocesan priests serving in the United States. He estimated that about 1,250 Irish-born priests were serving in the United States. He collected names of alumni of Irish seminaries who were in the United States, and 402 of them returned his questionnaires. Their mean age was 62.

Why had they come to the United States? Forty-three percent said they were assigned by their bishops to come here, while 57 percent had volunteered for service in an American diocese, usually because they had not been chosen by an Irish bishop for sponsorship in a seminary (Smith 2004, 75). This means that virtually all had been forced to leave Ireland or to seek support from outside Ireland for their seminary training. Were they treated differently by American Catholics because they were from Ireland? Fifty-one percent said yes:

> The priests were treated differently by non-Catholics and by other priests, particularly American-born priests. Time and time again in their answers the Irish priests mentioned the animosity held by American-born priests toward them. (2004, 84–85)

Here are typical comments by Smith's respondents:

> My opinion is that most parishioners in American parishes, at least in the Southeastern dioceses, would prefer an Irish priest to an American priest. I suspect the reason for it is that the Irish are more pastoral, less bureaucratic, more personal, less rational/academic. Of course it's quite chic in academe and among American women religious to be anti-Irish, but not so among ordinary parishioners. Being thus favored has its disadvantages however. Some Irish priests play the "Irish ticket" to a shameful degree, substituting charm for substance. (2004, 86)

> The people in parishes have been wonderful. Our biggest difficulty in the beginning was with the native clergy. They seemed to resent us, particularly if we got a promotion. Sometimes Americans of Irish descent may favor Irish-born priests, but generally speaking I do not think I am treated differently.

> The parishioners have been wonderful to me over the past forty-three years, no matter what nationality they happen to be. Unfortunately and sadly the same cannot be said about some native priests. We were "outsiders" when we came. This feeling is still present among some of the present generation. (2004, 87)

The Irish priests were overwhelmingly happy in their priesthood. Smith asked them about problems they were facing, and the main problems were overwork, loneliness, celibacy, and the shortage of clergy. Yet on balance they had high morale.

Smith concluded that the often-heard description today of F.B.I.'s in the United States—that they are ultraconservative—is unwarranted by the facts. Yes, they have been conservative on personal moral issues such as sex and marriage, but not on everything. Also, the view that Irish priests came to America reluctantly is unwarranted; the vast majority came willingly, with a strong sense of mission and hope for new possibilities here (2004, 118). True, many were homesick, and many found American ways difficult to accept. But the majority served with devotion, energy, and openness. They left a strong legacy of progressive activism with immigrants and labor unions.

As a postscript to this depiction of Irish-born priests, we should note that the heroic twentieth-century Irish era of missionary priests has ended. It is finished. Vocations dropped precipitously in Ireland in the 1980s and 1990s, and today the seminaries in Ireland no longer produce even enough priests for the Irish church. All but two seminaries in Ireland have closed due to lack of students (Smith 2004, 4). In 1997 there were only 119 seminarians preparing for the priesthood in Ireland. This sudden collapse of vocations was part of a broader breakdown of church authority in Ireland. Apparently underlying social pressures had been building in Ireland for several decades and had only been waiting for favorable political events to have an effect.

The Mid-Twentieth Century

The chronic shortage of American priests eased in the 1940s and 1950s. By this time American seminaries were well developed and filled with students. But American Catholics today often mistakenly take the immediate pre-Vatican II years—the forties and fifties—as representing all past history. No, those decades were unusual. They can be seen as a final golden age of the immigrant church, full of vigor and hope, well supplied with native-born seminarians. The longer-term American past saw shortages of American seminarians and endless efforts to recruit priests from Europe. The ratios of priests to laypersons from 1900 until today are shown in Table 1.1. American Catholicism had more priests in service, relative to laity, in 1940 and 1950 than at any time before or since. Since the 1970s the shortage of priests has intensified. An outcome of this history is that older American Catholics today remember the 1940s and 1950s and compare today with that blessed age when priests were everywhere.

Table 1.1
Ratio of Priests to Laypeople, 1900–2004

Year	Number of Priests	Millions of Catholics	Ratio of Priests to Laypeople
1900	11,987	12	1:1,001
1910	16,550	16	1:967
1920	21,019	20	1:951
1930	27,864	20	1:718
1940	35,839	22	1:614
1950	43,889	29	1:661
1960	54,682	42	1:768
1970	58,161	48	1:825
1980	58,398	50	1:856
1990	53,088	59	1:1,111
2000	45,699	60	1:1,313
2004	43,304	64	1:1,478

Data from Gerald Shaughnessy, *Has the Immigrant Kept the Faith?* (New York: Arno Press and *The New York Times* [1925] 1969); *Official Catholic Directory,* annual eds. (New Providence, NJ: P. J. Kenedy). Includes diocesan and religious priests.

Americans also seem to believe that this country has always been a source of missionaries to the rest of the world. We have encountered American Catholics who assume that this country has always been a resource for the growth of world Catholicism, including its ability to send priests to the world; therefore they feel embarrassed that today the United States needs to receive foreign priests to satisfy its own priestly needs. It is felt as a humiliation or loss of face. They ask: "How did it happen that our nation, which [they assume] has always given priests to missions to the poor countries, now needs to receive priests from those very same countries? What happened?"

This sentiment, although widespread, is based on myth and not fact, and it impedes the receptivity of foreign-born priests by many laypersons. People ask: "Why are they here? Aren't they needed in the mission fields?" A clarification of the facts, namely, that America has from the beginning relied on international priests, would help overcome this troublesome myth.

Throughout the 1980s pressures built up in American dioceses, due to the shortage of priests, to bring in more from overseas. Dioceses tried one thing and another. For example, in the early 1980s the Diocese of Rockville Centre became a leader in inviting Third World priests, and it incardinated forty-two international priests. Yet problems that created opposition emerged. The incoming priests often had serious problems with the English language, and they lacked knowledge of American culture. In 1986 the diocese, even though it faced a continuing priest shortage, decided to stop incardinating priests from other nations. As the director of personnel at the time said, "We get too much flak from our people, who can't understand them" (Hoge 1987, 118). The diocese instead put its energy into training lay ministers for parish leadership.

The 1999 Guidelines of the American Bishops

By the middle 1990s enough difficulties had arisen over international priests that the Bishops' Committee on Migration began an investigation and wrote a book of recommendations entitled *Guidelines for Receiving Pastoral Ministers in the United States,* published in 1999. The staff person in charge of producing the book was Aniedi Okure, O.P., a co-author of the present book. The forty-six-page report discussed the most vexing problems and how they could be alleviated. It begins by reciting the "difficulties" in the process of bringing in priests at the time—selection of candidates, processing immigration papers, determining the terms of service, providing orientation, finding suitable jobs and housing, making educational arrangements, and so on. It makes three overall recommendations: (a) the international priest needs an orientation to America before leaving home; (b) he needs at least two to three months to adjust to American society and culture before beginning his ministry here; and (c) he needs to get a letter of agreement or contract with the receiving bishop, specifying his position, salary, and benefits.

Regarding the process of recruiting, the report recommends that the American bishop make a written request to the diocesan bishop or major superior in the foreign country. Then the bishop or superior must nominate a specific priest and must vouch for his health, ability, experience, and character. The American bishop must state clearly that the priest will not be dependent on supplemental employment or solicitation of funds for his support during his stay in the United States, and he should state his diocese's policy regarding fundraising by individual priests. The receiving bishop and the priest should come to an understanding that the latter has come to serve the whole church and will not be relegated to serving only those who speak his native language.

Taking these measures would reduce the number of "freelance" priests who find their own way to the United States and then hunt around for a bishop who will take them, and it would reduce misunderstandings about finances and assignments.

The report recommends good orientation programs for the priests. Orientation lasting several days should take place in the country of origin and be devoted to providing information about American society. After the priest arrives in the United States, he should be given two to three months for initial adjustment, during which time the diocese should help him develop a personal support network of both native and foreign-born clergy, and he should enroll in classes in spoken English. He should be assigned a mentor for a period of at least three years. Twelve to eighteen months after arrival, another training program should be offered, covering the history of the American church, ministry in a multicultural church, the role of lay ministers, and other topics.

Some recommendations about orientation programs were specific. Large dioceses should sponsor their own orientation programs, normally once a year. Small dioceses with very few international priests should join with other dioceses or sponsor a shorter program. The initial orientation program should contain at least sixteen hours of program time, possibly over two to four days. It should cover practical topics, including bank accounts, driver's licenses, immigration status, shopping, social security, telephone, social norms such as tipping and table manners, gender rules, American holidays, sports, life in a rectory or religious community, expectations of the laity in a parish, diocesan rules, and professional boundaries.

In the six years since the *Guidelines* came out, the rules have been followed by more and more dioceses, according to reports from everyone we talked to. Today very few foreign-born priests are coming to the United States without explicit permission from their sending bishops or superiors, and agreements between the sending bishops or superiors and the receiving bishops are usually written out. In addition, since September 11, 2001, American immigration rules have tightened, making it more difficult and cumbersome to bring in priests. The process of bringing in international priests became much more regulated in the last four years. The development of orientation programs, however, is a task largely unfinished.

Vatican Instructions Regarding International Priests

The Vatican has recently issued several instructions regarding international priests. In 1980 Pope John Paul II issued "Norms for the Distribution of Priests," which asks that affluent nations share their priests with poorer nations and with mission territories.

In a 1990 encyclical entitled *Redemptoris Missio,* Pope John Paul II reiterated the need for more priests to serve in mission areas. Specifically, he encouraged bishops to offer some of their priests for temporary service in Africa.

In 2001 the Vatican Congregation for the Evangelization of Peoples issued norms governing diocesan priests serving abroad. These norms were written to counter a growing trend of priests moving from developing nations to Europe or North America for further studies or for special ministerial service, then to remain there and never go home. The reasons why priests from developing nations wanted to go abroad were well known and clearly stated in the document. Priests are motivated, in part, to move to wealthy nations for the economic opportunities there. The result is that too many priests move to Europe or North America to study, then make themselves available to the local bishops and soon overextend their stay, hoping to remain permanently. A certain number of them defy the commands of their home bishop to return to their native country. The sending bishops, due to the long distances and poor communication, in effect lose control of those priests.

The 2001 norms state that from now on, bishops in mission countries should choose the priests they will send abroad to pursue further studies. The bishops should designate the field of study for the priest, the faculty in which he will study, and the date of his definite return. A written agreement must be made between the bishop and the overseas institution in which the priest is to study, including clarification of his financial support. The receiving bishop is obligated to provide spiritual assistance to the priest, including help in incorporating him into the life of the presbyterate (Congregation for the Evangelization of Peoples 2001, arts. 1–7). These Vatican norms of 2001 were an attempt to counteract irregular and under-the-radar movements of priests from nation to nation.

This review of American history and of some Catholics' erroneous memories of that history will help us interpret the research on international priests today. The next chapter looks at the new studies.

Chapter 2

The New International Priests after 1985

To be a priest in America is indeed a challenge.
—A priest from the Philippines serving in New York

I see myself as bringing the gospel message to people other than mine. I am far from home, far from relatives, but not far from Christ and his message.
—A priest from Cameroon serving in Florida

Our 2004 surveys provide new information on the international priests in the United States. One survey asked all the dioceses and a hundred of the largest religious institutes about the numbers of international priests, about their policies, and about problems they face. The other asked a sample of international priests about their backgrounds, experiences, and recommendations. Details of both surveys are given in the Appendix (pp. 150–2).

Carrying out this project was an education in itself. The task was more difficult than we expected. First, nobody possessed lists of international priests that we could use for sampling, and nobody was even able to tell us how many priests from different nations were serving in the United States today. We had to piece together our sampling list. Later, when we mailed the questionnaires, the return rate was low, and when we interviewed a sample of the priests by phone, we found the majority to be cautious. This was not only because of English language difficulties but more often because of their fear of repercussions if they might say anything out of line. In enrolling priests for focus groups, we found that many were hesitant to talk to us. The Asians were the most circumspect. We did our best, but we are not sure we have captured a true representative sample of feelings of the international priests. Our mail survey has biases in that priests with poor English, priests afraid of surveys, and priests feeling insecure are underrepresented.

Numbers of International Priests

How many international priests are serving in the United States? CARA (Center for Applied Research in the Apostolate) estimated in 1999 that

7,600 foreign-born priests were serving in the United States at that time, or 16 percent of all priests (Froehle et al. 1999). In our 2004 survey of dioceses and religious institutes, we asked only about priests who began ministry in 1985 or later. The total reported was 4,499—4,006 diocesan and 493 religious priests. Since only 78 percent of the dioceses and 58 percent of the institutes responded, we estimate that if everyone had responded, the total would be about 5,700.[1] This estimate includes a probable double reporting of some religious priests (that is, reported by a diocese and also by a religious institute). Taking account of them, the total would be about 5,500; about 13 percent are religious priests and 87 percent are diocesan priests.

Of all priests in America who began ministry in 1985, the estimated percentage who are international is thus 16—the same figure as in the CARA estimate. Of the diocesan priests who began ministry in the United States in 1985 or later, about 17 percent are foreign-born; of the religious priests, about 9 percent.

The percentage of foreign-born seminary students in America today is higher. A 2004 study by CARA found that 22 percent of students in theology are foreign-born, and this figure is similar for diocesan and religious seminarians. The principal countries of origin are Mexico and Poland, followed by Colombia. Of these students, 84 percent expect to remain in the United States, and 16 percent expect to leave (CARA Report 2005).

Surveys of new ordinands have found that large percentages of them were born outside the United States. In 2003, 28 percent were born outside the United States; in 2004 it was 31 percent, and in 2005 it was 27 percent. Due to the upward trends among international seminarians and ordinands, we estimate that 16 or 17 percent of all priests in the nation today who began ministry in 1985 or later are foreign-born, and the percentage is gradually rising. The main countries of origin recently have been Vietnam and Mexico. Of all the new foreign-born ordinands, about 89 percent are diocesan and 11 percent are religious priests.

If we divide the total international priests by 19 (for the years 1985–2004), we get 289 beginning service and remaining here each year. Many others have come and gone in the meantime. Taking them into account, a better estimate of the number entering each year would be 380 to 400.[2]

1. The questionnaire asked the diocesan offices how many international priests were ministering full-time or part-time in their diocese, and the number reported certainly included some religious as well as diocesan priests. Using as an estimate that one-half of all religious priests were double-counted in this way, we adjusted our estimate from 5,700 to 5,500, and the percentage religious from 11 to 13. We believe these are the best possible estimates from available data.

2. We estimated that 5,500 are here in service, and about 1,500 have gone home since 1985. This gives us an estimate of 7,000 who began ministry since 1985.

How many were trained here? American seminaries are producing about 500 ordinations per year, of which about 28 percent are international, and of them 84 percent expect to remain here. That means 118 per year. If 380 to 400 international priests begin ministry each year, we calculate that in recent years about 30 percent of international priests beginning ministry were trained and ordained in the United States.

These international priests are not located randomly across the nation; rather, they are found in concentrations in several areas.[3] The main concentrations are in the Pacific coast area, the Southwest, Florida, and the greater New York area. The dioceses with the largest numbers, as far as we know, are Los Angeles (384), New York (278), Newark (235), Miami (200), and Chicago (174).

The religious institutes that have the most international priests, according to our information, are the Society of the Divine Word (57) and the Oblates of Mary Immaculate (42).

American Priests Serving Overseas

To provide context, we looked at how many priests from the United States are serving abroad. The most recent *U.S. Catholic Mission Handbook* (2004) lists 111 American-born diocesan priests and 1,420 American-born religious priests serving abroad. The religious orders with the largest numbers ministering abroad (including Puerto Rico) are:

Jesuits	265
Maryknoll	256
Oblates (all groups)	122
Franciscans (all groups)	77
Society of the Divine Word	67

These men are serving in all nations of the world, with the largest numbers in the Philippines, Brazil, Peru, Mexico, Japan, and Kenya. They tend to be older men. The average age of diocesan missionaries (including those serving in the United States as well as overseas) is fifty-nine. We have no information on how many of these men began their overseas ministries in 1985 or later, but probably it would be a little less than half, given their age today.

The number of American priests serving overseas is lower today than it was thirty years ago. The era of Americans going abroad for mission work had a slow start early in the century, but the numbers grew in the 1920s and

---

3. We divided the United States into four regions and found that 19 percent of the international priests are in the West and Mountain regions; 9 percent are in the Midwest (from North Dakota to Ohio); 27 percent are in the Northeast (Pennsylvania to Maine), and 45 percent are in the South and Southeast (Texas to Maryland).

then surged in the 1950s. The main destination of missionaries shifted from China to Oceania and Latin America after the Chinese communist takeover in 1949. In the 1950s Jesuits, Franciscans, Divine Word, and Maryknoll priests were the largest groups of missionaries. In 1960 diocesan priests in Boston founded the Society of St. James, which sent hundreds of missionaries from various dioceses to Latin America in succeeding decades; in its first twenty-five years it sent 270 to Bolivia, Peru, and Ecuador.

After the 1960s, missionary fervor in America declined. The peak year was 1968, when the total number of missionaries serving overseas, lay and ordained, was 9,655 (Dries 1998, 246). By today those numbers are down by half. Things have changed. Today the main sources of missionaries throughout the world are Asia, Africa, and the Pacific (Bevans and Schroeder 2004, 255).

Life Histories of the International Priests

The average age of international diocesan priests in 2004 was 47, and the average of the religious priests was 45. This makes them much younger than American priests, whose average age in 2001 was 59 for diocesan priests, 64 for religious priests, or 60 in all. Of all *non-retired* American priests in 2001, the average age was 55 for diocesan priests and 62 for religious priests. The international priests average about ten years younger.

We asked the international priests how long they expect to stay in the United States, and the vast majority said either "more than 5 years" or "uncertain"—73 percent of the diocesan priests and 77 percent of the religious. Only a small number expect to leave the United States in the next few years.

Are they incardinated in a diocese or affiliated with a religious institute? Of the diocesan priests, 34 percent said they were now incardinated, and 12 percent more said "I intend to be." Of the religious priests, 89 percent are affiliated with an institute here. (See Table A.2 in the Appendix, p. 154.)

Did these men complete their seminary training in the United States or in other nations? Mostly in other nations; only 19 percent of the diocesan priests and 23 percent of the religious completed their seminary studies here. Most were ordained in other countries, not in the United States; only 20 percent of the diocesan priests and 30 percent of the religious priests were ordained in this country.

We asked the priests if they were associated with any Catholic apostolic movements, for example, Focolare, the charismatic renewal, or the Neo-Catechumenate. Twenty-one percent of the diocesan priests and 14 percent of the religious priests said yes. Which movements? Most frequent was the charismatic renewal, followed by Focolare and Cursillos de Cristianidad. (See Table A.3, p. 155.)

What was the primary reason they came to the United States? We asked them to select one of five responses—studies; ministry; join family; refugee; or other. The most frequent by far was "ministry," checked by 61 percent of the diocesan priests and 61 percent of the religious. Second most frequent, but far behind, was "studies," checked by 18 percent of the diocesan priests and 14 percent of the religious. Eleven percent of the diocesan and 11 percent of the religious priests checked "refugee," and they were mainly from Vietnam, plus a few from Cuba. Only 4 percent of the diocesan and 9 percent of the religious priests checked "to join family." Not many are full-time students now—only 11 percent of the diocesan priests and 16 percent of the religious.

We asked, "Do you see yourself as a missionary within the Catholic Church?" Most said yes—86 percent of the diocesan and 90 percent of the religious priests.

Did these priests come to the U.S. at their own initiative, or were they sent by their bishop or religious superior? The most frequent response was "my bishop or religious superior," checked by 43 percent of the diocesan priests and 70 percent of the religious. Thirty-seven percent of the diocesan and 14 percent of the religious priests said "my initiative"; 19 percent of the diocesan and 11 percent of the religious priests said "initiated by the U.S. church."

How many of these priests are now naturalized citizens of the United States? Thirty-seven percent of the diocesan and 31 percent of the religious are, but a few more said "I intend to become naturalized"—15 percent of the diocesan and 13 percent of the religious.

Advanced Degrees

We asked, "Do you have an advanced degree other than the B.D., S.T.B., M.Div., or M.A. in theology?" Thirty-nine percent of the diocesan priests and 30 percent of the religious said yes. In what field? The fields most frequently given were philosophy and theology.

Where did they earn these advanced degrees? Forty percent of the diocesan priests and 39 percent of the religious priests earned their advanced degrees in the United States, 34 percent of the diocesan and 17 percent of the religious earned them in Europe (including Rome), and the rest on other continents.

Arrival in the United States

We asked numerous questions about the priests' experiences when they first arrived in the United States. Did they have a formal welcome by other priests or by their place of ministry? Yes. Sixty-four percent of the diocesan priests and 60 percent of the religious priests said this.

When they first arrived, did they attend any program for orientation or acculturation? For the majority, no. Only 33 percent of the diocesan priests and 35 percent of the religious said yes. If they had attended a program, which one or what kind? The most common were programs sponsored by their own diocese or order, English-language programs, or cultural programs of some kind. Only among the religious did a noteworthy number attend the nationally known acculturation programs sponsored by the Oblate School of Theology in San Antonio, by Maryknoll, or others. Forty-seven percent of the religious priests who had attended an orientation program had attended the Oblate program or the Maryknoll program.

How long did the orientation programs last? Forty-nine percent of the diocesan priests and 33 percent of the religious said "less than two weeks"; another 25 percent of the diocesan priests and 33 percent of the religious said "one to six months." This question is ambiguous, since many programs meet occasionally, not continually, over a one-year or two-year period, and we are uncertain how priests who took part in those programs reported the length of the programs. (See Table A.4, p. 157.)

Was the orientation program helpful? Ninety-six percent of the diocesan priests and 100 percent of the religious priests said yes. Why was it helpful? We asked the men to write in responses, and they gave three types of answers. Most frequent was "improved cultural understanding and reduced culture shock." Second most frequent: "better understanding of the local diocese or parish." Third most frequent: "improved language skills or preaching skills." We consider these findings to be central to our research project: *virtually all the priests who attended orientation programs praised the programs.*

We asked, "Did you have a formal mentor or formal support network during your first three years in the United States?" Thirty-three percent of the diocesan priests and 51 percent of the religious said yes. We asked them to describe the mentorship or support network. Most commonly it was done by priests from the diocese, the deanery, or congregation, the vicar for clergy, a spiritual director, or the local pastor and staff.

Finally, did the diocese or religious community help these priests with immigration problems? Sixty-two percent of the diocesan priests and 72 percent of the religious said yes.

Current Ministry

Next we asked seven questions about these priests' ministry today. First, "Do you have an official assignment from the diocese or religious institute you work for?" Mostly yes—88 percent of the diocesan and 88 percent of the religious priests. We asked what their primary ministry is. Most commonly the men are parochial vicars (57 percent of the diocesan priests, 41 percent of the religious), but smaller numbers are pastors (19 percent of the diocesan, 25 percent of the religious) or chaplains or spiritual directors (19 percent of the diocesan, 23 percent of the religious). A few are teachers, formation directors, or part-time ministers.

If a diocesan priest is not incardinated, is there a letter of agreement between the bishop of his home diocese and the bishop in the United States? Eighty-three percent said yes. If a religious priest is not affiliated with an institute in the U.S., is there a letter of agreement between his home provincial and the diocese in the United States? Again yes—83 percent.

Questions about Money

We asked two questions about money. First, "Do you regularly send money from your personal income to help support your family in your home country?" Forty-nine percent of the diocesan priests and 13 percent of the religious said yes. The difference between 49 and 13 is partly explained by the different financial systems. Diocesan priests receive paychecks personally, while most religious priests have their salaries sent to their religious communities, and they live on stipends from their provinces; thus diocesan priests commonly have more money available. We are uncertain of the details.

Two knowledgeable persons told us that they do not believe the 49 percent and 13 percent figures found in our survey. They said the truth is a higher percentage. These persons explained that in many cultures any member of a family who has a good income is seriously obligated to send money to the others, and certainly obligated to help his parents. Thus it is totally normal that international priests in the United States would be sending money home to their parents.

The second question asked, "Since you began ministry in the United States, have you raised money from parishioners to support your diocese, religious order, or mission project in your home country?" Not many. Only 19 percent of the diocesan priests and 11 percent of the religious said they had. (See Table A.5, p. 160.) Raising money openly for one's home country is much different from sending money home from one's paycheck, and, as we will see, American dioceses discourage it.

Relations with Other Priests

Because we had heard reports of poor relations with American priests, we asked four questions. (See Table 2.1.) At the top of the table we see that the majority of priests feel totally accepted by other priests. Very few said they did not feel accepted.

Do they attend general gatherings of priests in their diocese? Fifty-seven percent of the diocesan priests and 57 percent of the religious said they always did, and most of the rest said they sometimes did. Do they meet with other priests from their country of origin or cultural group? Yes, 82 percent of the diocesan priests and 66 percent of the religious said "regularly" or "occasionally."

Table 2.1
Relationships with Other Priests (in Percents)

		Diocesan	Religious
Do you now feel accepted by other priests in your diocese or religious institute?			
	Yes, totally	58	75
	Partly	39	25
	No	3	0
Whether diocesan or religious, do you attend the general gatherings of priests in the diocese where you are ministering?			
	Always	57	57
	Sometimes	40	34
	Never	4	9
How often do you attend gatherings of priests from your country of origin or your cultural group?			
	Regularly	36	20
	Occasionally	46	46
	Never	11	20
	Not yet	8	15
Have you ever felt that you were assigned to a parish or ministry that other priests do not want?			
	Yes	16	13

How many feel that they were assigned to a parish or ministry that other priests did not want? Only 16 percent of the diocesan priests and 13 percent of the religious feel this way. We asked for details, and in the written-in reports the men told of being assigned to poor or multicultural parishes or to hospital ministries that the American priests didn't want. If the priests' responses represent their true sentiments, ill feelings toward American priests are not widespread. We will return to this topic in chapter 7.

Happiness

How happy are these priests with their lives and ministry? (See Table 2.2.) The priests are happiest with their sacramental and liturgical ministry. They are fairly happy with their personal spiritual life and the conditions for their ministry. The diocesan priests (but not the religious) are less happy with their present living situation, and all the priests are less than happy with their financial situation. All are *unhappy* with the image of the Catholic priesthood among the American public today.

Table 2.2
Measures of Happiness (in Percents)

	Diocesan	Religious
What is your happiness with the following specific conditions? How happy are you with: (Percent saying "Very happy")		
Your sacramental and liturgical ministry	46	38
Your personal spiritual life	29	31
Conditions for ministry in your diocese or religious institute	23	38
Your present living situation	21	40
Your present financial situation	16	21
The image of the Catholic priesthood in the American public today	5	2

In the questionnaire we asked about specific problems facing these priests. We stated, "There are many problems which face priests today. How important are the following problems *to you* on a day-to-day basis?" See Table 2.3, which shows the top eight out of the sixteen topics listed in the questionnaire.

Table 2.3

"There are many problems which face priests today. How important are the following problems to you *on a day-to-day basis?" (Top eight in the percent saying "a great problem for me personally.")*

	Diocesan	Religious
Loneliness of priestly life.	10	19
Too much work.	7	17
The way authority is exercised in the church.	5	17
Unrealistic demands and expectations of lay people.	7	7
Uncertainty about the future of the church.	6	7
Theological change in the concept of the priesthood.	6	6
Lack of opportunity for personal fulfillment.	2	7
Relationships with superiors or pastor.	4	4

The biggest single problem facing these priests is "the loneliness of priestly life." It is followed by "too much work," "the way authority is exercised in the church," "unrealistic demands and expectations of laypeople," "uncertainty about the future of the church," and "theological change in the concept of the priesthood." The religious priests reported more problems than did the diocesan priests. We wondered, do they really feel more problems, or were they more forthright in filling out the questionnaire? Our advisors said that we should believe that the religious priests actually do feel more problems, partly because they have less interaction with American priests.

The top four items in Table 2.3 were also the top four in a survey of all priests in the United States done in 2001 (Hoge and Wenger 2003, 32). The only difference was that loneliness was in first place for the international priests but much lower (fourth place) for all American priests. It seems that the stresses felt by international priests are similar to stresses felt by American priests, except that loneliness is more acute among the international ones.

Recommendations by the Priests

What would these priests recommend to help them in their ministries in the United States? We asked them to write in their recommendations, and later we coded them topic by topic. (See Table A.6, p. 162.) By far the most common recommendation was that the church should provide them acculturation training, including instruction in English. *This is the main recommendation from international priests for the American church today.*

Four other recommendations were also mentioned repeatedly: (1) establish periodic gatherings and support groups; (2) assure equal treatment to international priests, with no discrimination; (3) provide more support from the diocese; and (4) provide clearer rules and guidance.

The written comments on the surveys tell us more. Under the rubric of providing more acculturation and language training, the priests told us:

> Provide a good program of orientation about ministry in the U.S., utilizing the experience of foreign-born priests who have been here and done well. This is not just a matter of teaching the theory of acculturation but a matter of lived experience. (Nigeria)

> I believe the priests need a mentor, someone who understands this culture and theirs. (Nigeria)

> Help them out with English; provide an English tutor; make them feel welcome, especially from the priests they work with. (Vietnam)

> I recommend that a consultation of all priests born in other countries in the diocese or vicariate take place to discuss this issue. A good acculturation program should be provided by the diocese. And a mentoring program. (Philippines)

On the topic of periodic gatherings and support groups:

> Have a local/diocesan level organization meeting every quarter or bi-monthly to support each other. (Ghana)

> There should be a kind of general gathering to share experiences in the ministry and hopefully to find support from other non-U.S.-born priests. (Philippines)

> A get-together of priests of one's country could be organized to keep our spirit alive. (India)

On assuring equal treatment for foreign-born priests:

> The foreign-born should be allowed to function as competent priests. Many American priests, even the obviously ignorant ones, look down on foreign

priests as less competent and less well-trained. Nothing could be further from the truth. Most foreign priests are far better trained and far more competent in parish work. (Nigeria)

Outside priests in many of the U.S. dioceses are not treated equally. I worked 1½ years in the Archdiocese of ____, and my colleagues and I from outside the U.S. had the same treatment there. Often discouraged! (India)

Treat them with respect, as equals. Learn about their cultural background. American-born priests should go for pastoral ministry in other countries once in five years for at least a month. (India)

On the recommendation for more support from the diocese:

Foreign priests need to feel welcomed and informed about American culture, but most important, they need emotional, spiritual, and financial support from their American peers. (Brazil)

I think priests born in other countries need to be accepted and given an opportunity to share their cultural experiences with priests in the United States. (Nigeria)

I can't understand the American priests, because I was not born in America. I just want that we take enough time to understand each other. (Korea)

On the request for clearer rules and guidance:

It would be very helpful and advantageous if there was someone to guide and advise us. I was unaware of where to get help so that I could apply for a clergy visa and green card. Unfortunately I was misguided, and after sending an application in October, I was told that I had been given the wrong form. I had to re-apply and now after eight months I still do not have any of these credentials. (Poland)

The priests should be given a time for acculturation. This does not only mean learning the language but also most importantly the way things are done in the church in the U.S. (Congo)

Give them a manual of diocesan rules and regulations, rights and duties, and social etiquette. Have regular or occasional meetings with the local bishop. Some level of representation in the administrative organs of the diocese. (Nigeria)

The Survey of Dioceses and Religious Institutes

In our survey we asked the dioceses and religious institutes about their policies and programs. Do they have programs of orientation for international priests? (See Table 2.4.) About half said they have orientation programs for foreign-born priests, helping them with language training and helping them become better acquainted with other priests. The majority have programs for helping foreign-born priests with immigration procedures. Since the wording in the questionnaire was not specific, we don't know how extensive or serious the programs are.

Table 2.4
Programs of Dioceses and Institutes (in Percents)

	Dioceses	Religious Institutes
Does your diocese or religious institute have the following: (Percent "Yes")		
A program of orientation for priests from other countries	51	33
A program for helping priests from other countries with English language training	54	46
A program to help priests from other countries become acquainted with other priests	49	38
A program for helping priests from other countries with immigration procedures	78	59

Do the dioceses and religious institutes make special efforts to maintain contact with non-incardinated and non-affiliated priests working with them? In most cases no. They merely use their regular means of communication with priests. Yet 12 percent of the dioceses and 12 percent of the religious institutes said they have special visitations or orientations. (See Table A.8, p. 164.)

If a priest from another country is working in full-time pastoral ministry but is not incardinated, does he receive a salary and is he included in the health plan? Usually yes. Is there a letter of agreement between the local diocesan bishop and the sending bishop or religious superior? Ninety-two percent of the dioceses and 79 percent of the religious institutes said yes. Is there financial provision for his training? Yes, for 61 percent of the dioceses and 80 percent of the religious institutes. Is a priest designated to be his mentor? Thirty-seven percent of the dioceses said yes, as did 54 percent of the religious institutes. (See Table A.9, p. 165.)

We asked the diocesan and religious leaders what their main challenges have been in recent years with regard to foreign-born priests. We categorized the responses under ten headings. The most numerous by far were "poor English-language pronunciation; refusal to learn English" and "cultural insensitivity." (See Tables A.10 and A.11, pp. 166 and 167.) Two other topics were also named, but much less frequently: "different ecclesiology and problems of accepting leadership of the laity" and "treatment of women." These reports by diocesan and religious officials closely match the problems we encountered in our personal interviews (as we will see in chapter 5), and they are the main problem areas with international priests today.

Summary

Our two surveys in 2004 furnish a comprehensive view of the current situation regarding international priests in America. The value of these surveys is that they have generalizing power for seeing the total picture. In chapter 3 we will continue to look at the total picture, this time of the overall distribution of priests around the world. Then in chapters 4 and 5 we will look at the arguments pro and con about bringing in international priests.

Chapter 3

The Global Brain Drain
and Distribution of Priests

Over the past century the center of gravity in the Christian world has shifted inexorably southward, to Africa, Asia, and Latin America. Already today, the largest Christian communities on the planet are to be found in Africa and Latin America. *—Philip Jenkins*

To comprehend today's movement of priests from nation to nation, we need to explain more about the economic context. Pervasive pressures affecting churches and priests go far to explain the international movements of priests. Most basic is the global brain drain.

The Global Brain Drain

The movement of priests from poor nations to rich nations would seem to be one facet of the global brain drain. The direction of movement of personnel and the timing are similar. Yet Catholic priests are not the same as other professionals, so we need to inquire whether pressures producing the overall global brain drain go far to explain the movement of Catholic priests.

Let us recall the basic contours of the brain drain. It came to worldwide attention in the 1960s and 1970s, when newly independent nations were sending thousands of young persons to Europe and North America for advanced training. Many of these people did not return home. Salaries, opportunities, research grants, and access to the latest technology were so much better in the wealthy nations that the professionals stayed on, even when their governments tried hard to lure them back. A new factor is that in recent decades more and more professionals were trained at home in the developing nations—not just in Europe and North America—as universities in many nations were improving. This did not seem to have affected the brain drain, since graduates of universities in the new developing nations world have been shown to be just as likely to emigrate as graduates of European and North American universities (Glaser 1978).

Beginning in the 1970s, the movement of professionals and technical experts to Europe and North America accelerated, and it has continued to grow decade by decade. Ease of travel and communications, plus active recruiting by the wealthy nations, are behind the increase. Also, methods and standards of professional practice are becoming more and more similar in the world, so that, for example, a well-trained doctor, nurse, or scientist can quickly adapt to work in a different nation. The brain drain is certain to grow (Asmar 2003).

Salary differences are important. The average doctor in the United States earns thirty-one times as much as a doctor in Zambia does. Even minimum wage jobs, which pay $5.15 per hour in the United States, are alluring to people in Africa, where two-thirds of the population live on less than sixty dollars a month, according to the United Nations (Africa News 2003). In Kenya, beginning annual salaries for qualified persons are in the range of $1,500 to $2,500 for secondary teachers and nurses and $12,000 to $15,000 for doctors and engineers. Teachers from the Philippines working in the United States can expect to earn over $30,000 a year, compared with $5,000 at home (Stalker 2001). An Afro-Arab conference in 2003 observed that 54 percent of doctors, 26 percent of engineers, and 17 percent of scientists graduating from Arab and African universities migrate to Europe, the United States, and Canada (Asmar 2003). A 2003 report gives details:

> A World Bank report said in 1990 that there was one doctor to 22,970 people in Ghana, as against 1 to 420 in the United States and 1 to 810 in the United Kingdom. While one physician per 10,000 is required for minimal health interventions, the Ghana Medical Association said that as many as 600 medical practitioners from the country were practicing in New York. . . . The situation is no different in Benin, with more Benin doctors said to be working in France than in the West African country itself. (Ejime 2003)

A recent report based on United Nations data stated that 50 percent of medical doctors, 23 percent of engineers, and 15 percent of scientists from Arab nations are lost every year to Europe and North America (Asmar 2003). This entails an economic loss to the developing nations, since the nations have invested a lot in educating the young men and women, and when they leave, the recipient states do not need to fork out the costs of educating them.

Can the global brain drain be reversed? Yes, in a few situations. It has been reversed recently in the case of computer specialists returning to India, Taiwan, and South Korea. The main reason for this is the outsourcing of high-tech work to companies in developing nations; jobs in that field are flowing from America to Asia. China has had some success in luring technically trained Chinese who were educated overseas to come back to work in its high-tech development zones (Herbert and Guy 2003).

Otherwise, except for a few high-tech situations, the brain drain has never been reversed. Most efforts by national governments, foundations, and other organizations to stop it have failed. As a result, the brain drain is bigger today than ever (*New York Times,* August 19, 2004). Any serious effort to stem the tide will call for international organizations and agreements.

Is the movement of priests just one more instance of the brain drain? Largely, but not entirely. Priests, unlike other professionals, are not free to pick up and move from one nation to another. Whether they are diocesan or religious, priests need the permission of their bishops or provincials to emigrate. Also, priests respond to a different set of motivators. They have devoted their lives to the service of Jesus Christ, and monetary wealth is not a major life goal. We admit that motivations are difficult to fathom in any human being, but we believe that priests are relatively less influenced by money and more influenced by opportunities for spreading the gospel, work conditions, and the needs of their dioceses or religious orders.

Even though a high income may seem unpriestly as a motivator to move overseas, we should remember that priests in the United States receives much higher stipends than priests in developing nations, and many priests from poor countries send money to their families and to their dioceses. As we saw in chapter 2, 49 percent of the international diocesan priests and 13 percent of the international religious priests in the United States are sending money home to their families (and we noted that the true figures are possibly higher).

The brain-drain analogy is weak in another respect, namely, that over half of the priests who come to the United States eventually return home. We lack specific data on the percentage who do so, but our survey and our personal experience convince us that over half go back at some time. If they return home soon, it mitigates the overall loss to their home church. Other professions are different; the prospect of returning home soon is lower for doctors or engineers, who are more likely to relocate permanently in the West.

A crucial question remains: Is a brain drain of priests, although distinctive, good for world Catholicism? Is this something the Catholic Church should happily take part in, or should it take measures to stop it? In other professions, such as medicine, it has been proven, as we noted, that the poor nations are further impoverished by the departure of trained personnel. In the priesthood we believe the same is usually true, but it depends on how long the priest is gone. If a priest immigrates to Europe or America for a limited number of years and then returns home, the cost to his country entailed in his absence is partly offset by the valuable experience he has gained. Yet even with this in mind, we believe that the movement of priests to Europe and America is unjust to the poor nations. At least the costs of educating the priests, costs that were borne by the dioceses and religious orders in poor nations, should somehow be reimbursed.

Can anything be done? Maybe. It would require action by the central authorities of world Catholicism to restrain Catholics in the wealthy nations from acting solely out of their own self-interest. To illustrate, we point to the letter from the Vatican Congregation for the Evangelization of Peoples issued in June 2001, signed by Cardinal Jozef Tomko. The letter aimed to "counteract the prevalent trend of a certain number of diocesan priests who . . . want to leave their own country and reside in Europe or North America, often with the intention of further studies or for other reasons that are not actually missionary" (no. 3). Anyone close to the situation knows that many priests from poor nations have been trying every possible way to get to Europe or North America, either with their bishop's permission or without, and thousands stay. The letter of Cardinal Tomko said that if a bishop agrees to send a priest abroad for further training, he needs to spell out with the priests all the details ahead of time—the field of study, the university where the priest will enroll, and the date of definite return. This rule is a first small step.

An Instance of Outsourcing

As wages rise in the modern industrial nations, more and more nontechnical jobs are being transferred to developing nations. For example, garments are sewn and shoes are produced mostly in Asian factories today, not in Europe or North America. This process is called "outsourcing." The *New York Times* (Rai 2004) reported that with Catholic clergy in short supply in the United States, Canada, and Europe, priests in India are picking up some of their work.

In Kerala, the state of India with millions of Catholics, priests are receiving Mass intentions from overseas. The Masses are conducted in Malayalam, the native language, and the intention, often for the soul of a deceased person or for a sick relative, or thanks for a favor received, is announced. The requests are forwarded to Kerala's churches mostly through the Vatican, bishops, or religious orders. One bishop in Kerala said that his diocese received an average of 350 Mass intentions a month from overseas, most of which were passed on to needy priests. This practice is several decades old.

In Kerala's churches Masses for a special intention are said for a donation amounting to 90 U.S. cents, whereas a Mass stipend from the United States typically amounts from five to ten U.S. dollars. The money is a welcome supplement to priests' financial support. The practice is not widely known about in the United States and Europe. Some Catholics are reportedly shocked by this outsourcing of Masses, while others seem to accept it as a way to help priests in poor nations. In any case, we should recall that the practice has been going on for years.

We turn next to a related question, that of the deployment of priests in the world.

The Global Distribution of Priests

THE CHALLENGE BY PHILIP JENKINS

A fundamental challenge was made by historian Philip Jenkins in his 2002 book *The Next Christendom,* in which he argued that the Catholic Church is acting illogically and unreasonably. Catholicism is growing vigorously in Africa, Asia, and Latin America at the same time that it is stagnant in Europe. The future of world Catholicism lies in Africa, Asia, and Latin America! In Jenkins' words, "Christianity is going south" (p. 3). As a part of that, Asia and Africa are now fertile grounds for vocations.

Jenkins points out that future Catholic growth will be largely in urban areas of Asia, Africa, and Latin America. Therefore any far-sighted Catholic world leader would invest his resources to baptize and catechize the burgeoning populations ready to become Catholics in those regions. Yet when it comes to the availability of priests, the situation is just the opposite:

> It almost seems as if the church has scientifically assigned its resources to create the minimum possible correlation between priests and the communities that need them most. The Devil himself could scarcely have planned it better. . . . The Northern world, Europe and North America, presently accounts for 35 percent of Catholic believers and 68 percent of priests; Latin America has 42 percent of believers but only 20 percent of the priests. In terms of the ratio of priests to faithful, the Northern world is four times better supplied with clergy than the global South. (p. 213)

Jenkins recalls the endless complaints in Europe and North America about the priest shortage today, but he points out that the situation is much grimmer in Africa and Latin America. Many Catholic parishes in Brazil, for example, have fifty thousand members, and it is in countries like Brazil that future growth is certain to occur. Why would the Catholic Church be bringing priests from Africa, Latin America, and Asia to Europe and the United States when exactly the opposite *should be* the policy? Why are American bishops bringing priests from developing nations to the United States rather than sharing their priests with countries having fewer priests but more prospects for growth? "Viewed in a global perspective," Jenkins says, "such a policy can be described at best as painfully short-sighted, at worst as suicidal for Catholic fortunes" (p. 214).

APPRAISAL OF JENKINS' ARGUMENT

Jenkins provides no detailed statistics about the number of priests in various nations, but Vatican reports provide data for evaluating his argument. We have compared worldwide data for two years, 1985 and the latest available, which is 2002. Table 3.1 shows the growth in baptized Catholics and the number of Catholics per priest in seventeen continents and nations, along with the gross national product per capita of each.

Table 3.1
GNP per Capita (in 2002 dollars)[1]
Baptized Member Growth and Numbers of Catholics per Priest for
Selected Countries and Regions, 1985 and 2002[2]

Region	Country	GNP per Capita 2002	% Membership Growth 1985–2002	Catholics per Priests 1985	Catholics per Priests 2002
	United States	36,110	+23	936	1,375
All Europe		**17,730**	**+1**	**1,197**	**1,374**
	Ireland	29,570	+22	647	901
	Poland	10,450	+6	1,707	1,323
	Spain	21,210	+2	1,194	1,426
All East Asia		**5,973**	**+54**	**2,651**	**2,473**
	India	2,650	+33	1,005	834
	Indonesia	3,070	+55	2,348	2,048
	Republic of Korea	16,960	+223	1,539	1,422
	Philippines	4,450	+42	8,859	8,454
	Vietnam	2,300	n/a	n/a	2,071
All Africa		**2,100**	**+89**	**4,024**	**4,694**
	Nigeria	800	+243	4,538	4,227
All Mexico, Central America, Caribbean		**7,240**	**+27**	**7,707**	**6,944**
All South America		**6,970**	**+27**	**6,935**	**7,138**
	Brazil	7,450	+24	8,724	8,808
	Colombia	6,150	+42	4,960	4,890

1. *2004 World Population Data Sheet* (GNI PPP per capita, 2002). Washington, DC: PRB, 2004.

2. *Statistical Yearbook of the Church,* Civitas Vaticana: Typis Polyglottis Vaticanis, 1985, 2002.

Worldwide, the number of baptized Catholics grew 26 percent between 1985 and 2002, according to Vatican statistics. During the same years, we may note in passing, world population growth was 29 percent, with the greatest increase in Asia and Africa. The greatest growth in Catholic membership since 1985 has been in Africa and Asia, as Jenkins rightly pointed out. The United States, Central America, and South America grew also, but more slowly. Europe did not grow.

By comparing the first and second columns, we see that generally the lower the gross national product per capita, the greater the Catholic growth. South Korea is a major exception, since it has a GNP per capita of 16,960 dollars, yet a very high growth rate. Otherwise, Catholic growth is greatest in the poorer nations.

The last column in Table 3.1 reports that the wealthy nations, with one exception, have many more priests than the poor nations. In the United States there are 1,375 Catholics per priest, and in Europe it is 1,374 per priest. Contrast this with South America with 7,138 per priest, Central America and the Caribbean with 6,944 per priest, and Africa with 4,694 per priest. In the entire world there are 2,642 Catholics per priest. Figure 3.1 depicts the pattern.

Figure 3.1
Number of Catholics per Priest, 2002

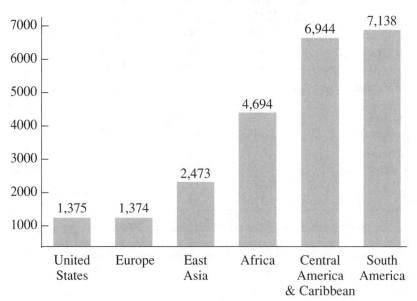

The exception is India, where an unusually large number of priests are available. The ratio of Catholics to priests in India is as low as anywhere in the world, even though India ranks low in wealth. One possible reason why India is an exception is that the nation has very few Catholics, and the Catholics it has are largely in the southern province of Kerala. The citizens of Kerala are the best-educated and wealthiest in India and are unusual in other ways too. In an attempt to understand what is happening in India, we consulted several experts. They proposed theories, but nobody had decisive information on why India is unique. They pointed out that India has relatively few Catholics and that the subcontinent is diverse from region to region. Even within Catholicism, they noted, India has an unusually large number of specific rites that have been passed down for a millennium. They suggested that for cultural reasons priests are looked upon differently in India than elsewhere, so that the laity contribute more money for priests' training and support. They pointed to the dynamics of the Indian caste system. In the end we found no convincing explanation.

The contrast between the wealthy and poor nations in Table 3.1 is slightly overstated in one respect, namely, in the wealthy nations a proportion of the priests are retired and not available for service, while this is less true in the developing nations. The difference occurs because of the recency of the ordinations in the developing nations and the younger age of the priests. For example, in 2001, 16 percent of all diocesan and religious priests in the United States were retired (Hoge and Wenger 2003, 200), whereas in Nigeria only 1 to 3 percent of the priests today are retired.

Table 3.1 upholds Jenkins' argument well. Catholic growth is occurring in the poor continents, and the concentrations of priests are in the wealthy continents. Yet another factor we need to consider is the trend in seminarians. It is described in Table 3.2, which shows changes in the number of seminarians between 1985 and 2002. There was a drop-off in seminarians in the United States and Europe but growth in the rest of the world. Africa had a very remarkable growth of 122 percent, and East Asia had a growth of 71 percent. Central America, the Caribbean, and South America had moderately strong growth.

The case of Nigeria is illustrative. Until the 1960s the church in Nigeria depended on foreign missionaries, but beginning in that decade, seminaries began opening and by today produce more priests than the nation can support. The Nigerian seminaries continue to expand today, and they envision preparation of priests for the entire continent. Ordinations in Nigeria took place mostly in the last two decades, and the priests are much younger than the priests in the United States.

Future vocations serving the entire world will be coming largely from Asia, Africa, and Latin America—no longer from Europe and North America.

The era of missionary priests from countries like Ireland and Poland scattering to all corners of the globe is now over. In this new century Nigeria and India will be the equivalent of Ireland in the early twentieth century as a provider of priests. We are entering a new era in world Catholicism.

The last column in Table 3.2 shows that the number of Catholics per seminarian in 2002 varies greatly. For the entire world the figure is 9,455. Five countries have far more than average numbers of seminarians—India, Indonesia, South Korea, Vietnam, and Nigeria. These, with the exception of South Korea, are poor nations that cannot financially maintain large numbers of priests, so in the future they will have priests available for service in other nations.

To summarize: Philip Jenkins' challenge is correct, with two provisos. One is that seminary enrollments are growing in much of the world; Asia and Africa will be producing more and more priests as the years go on, and the shortage in those continents will be eased. The second is that world Catholicism needs a flow of *money* as well as a flow of priests from north to south. Without more money, an increase in priests in the poor nations will be impossible.

We have been assuming to this point that the priest shortage can be measured more or less accurately by statistics showing the number of Catholics per priest. But the concept "shortage" has subjective as well as objective dimensions. This needs to be explained.

A "Shortage" of Priests

A "shortage" of priests can be defined in three ways. The first is the statistic showing the number of Catholics per priest, as we have seen in Table 3.1. This measure is objective and simple.

The second depends on the *feeling* of Catholics in one area or other that a priest shortage exists. For anyone to feel that there is a shortage, he or she would have had to experience a situation of more priests, either in the same nation at an earlier time or in another nation. It is instructive to remember that in the United States there was no discussion of a "priest shortage" until the 1980s, when alarmed voices in the Catholic community pointed out that fewer priests were available than was the case ten or twenty years earlier. That is, a *recent change* in the availability of priests produced a feeling that a shortage had arisen.

The same kind of feeling could arise from an individual's experience of living in a different country where the availability of priests was higher. A Catholic who has always lived in Mexico or Brazil would say "What shortage?" even in the face of compelling statistical evidence of having far lower numbers of priests, since he or she never knew anything else and thinks that the present situation is normal.

Table 3.2

Increase or Decrease in Seminarians for Selected Countries and Regions, 1985, 2002[1]

Region	Country	Seminarians 1985	Seminarians 2002	Percentage Change	Catholics per Seminarian 1985	Catholics per Seminarian 2002
	United States	7,131	5,169	-28	7,438	12,663
All Europe		**28,610**	**25,023**	**-13**	**9,719**	**11,186**
	Ireland	1,283	206	-84	3,077	23,456
	Poland	8,089	6,737	-17	4,331	5,489
	Spain	3,346	2,634	-21	11,292	14,593
All East Asia		**15,495**	**26,432**	**71**	**4,508**	**4,065**
	India	6,334	11,574	83	2,037	1,478
	Indonesia	1,585	2,831	79	2,588	2,252
	Republic of Korea	1,253	1,637	31	1,550	2,642
	Philippines	4,985	6,688	34	9,209	9,728
	Vietnam	n/a[2]	1,878		n/a	2,955
All Africa		**10,025**	**22,210**	**122**	**7,248**	**6,188**
	Nigeria	2,029	4,689	131	3,552	3,738
All Mexico, Central America, Caribbean		**7,106**	**9,766**	**37**	**16,503**	**15,251**
All South America		**14,537**	**22,378**	**54**	**16,573**	**13,702**
	Brazil	5,912	9,725	64	20,311	15,355
	Colombia	2,673	4,840	81	10,172	7,996

1. *Statistical Yearbook of the Church.* Civitas Vaticana: Typis Polyglottis Vaticanis, 1985, 2002.
2. n/a = not available

The point here is that "shortage" has decisive subjective elements, and we can only understand statements about priest shortages when we take into account both objective and subjective conditions. In the real world of decision-making in the church, subjective feelings are the most telling. But Catholics everywhere would benefit from seeing the availability of priests in global terms. It would aid them in understanding global Catholicism, even though it would not mollify American Catholics unhappy because priests and priestly services are in shorter supply than they were recently.

This argument is sometimes used to interpret the statistical evidence of a priest shortage in Latin America. One priest told us that even though the ratio of laity to priests is much higher in Latin American than in the United States, the statistics were irrelevant, since the type of Catholicism that has evolved in Latin America *does not require* as many priests. This person said that Latin Americans have developed a family-based or home-based Catholicism more than a parish-based Catholicism, with religion being taught by mothers and grandmothers. Nobody feels a need for weekly Mass attendance or frequent reception of the sacraments. An American missionary in Brazil told us that in Brazil there is less concern about a "priest shortage" than there is in the United States.

The third definition of "shortage" is more abstract yet equally pertinent. It defines "shortage" as not having enough priests to do what is needed. In a country such as Nigeria, Ghana, or India, with millions of people showing signs of readiness for evangelization to Catholicism, additional priests are needed to do mission work. This understanding of shortage is assumed in Jenkins' argument that Catholic priests should be deployed as much as possible in Asia, Latin America, and Africa in view of the obvious opportunities for growth there, in contrast to the less hopeful mission opportunities in places like the Netherlands, Germany, or the United States.

Using this definition, one can only conclude that the whole world has a priest shortage! We agree. What Catholic community wouldn't benefit from having more active, capable, devoted priests working for it? In much of the world the harvest is ready, but laborers are needed. If suitable candidates would come forth, why shouldn't we *double* the number of priests in the world? It would advance the cause of Christianity. The only limit in such a circumstance would be the money needed to support them. Put plainly: How many jobs for priests could we create in each country, given the money available? And how much money would Catholics in affluent nations be willing to send to poorer nations to support more priests there?

A further conundrum arises when we note that the laity-per-priest ratio in American Protestant denominations is much different from that in Catholicism. For Catholics in America in 2001, the figure was 1,375 laity per priest. For American Protestants the figure was much lower—in 2003, between 270 and 300 laity per minister. The greater numbers of clergy in American Protestant churches are made possible by a higher level of financial contributions by members. In the late 1990s, for every $100 dollars a typical Catholic household gave to its parish, a typical Protestant household gave $303 (Hoge et al. 1996, 32). American Protestants want more clergy and are willing to pay for them. This raises a question: Would Catholics in America contribute more if it meant they could have more priests?

With this background information, we can begin to understand the arguments being made today for and against bringing in more international priests to the United States. The next two chapters outline the arguments.

Chapter 4

The Arguments for Bringing in International Priests

Some of our pastors say, "We need priests, so we'll take anyone!"
—A vicar for priests in the South

I'm concerned about the increasing U.S.A. narrowness and provincialism. This is not something new. Most U.S.A. people speak one language, and we think that if someone doesn't speak English, they're stupid!
—An American nun teaching in acculturation programs

On November 14, 1997, Richard P. McBrien, professor of theology at Notre Dame, wrote a column in the *National Catholic Reporter* entitled "Importing Priests to U.S. a Poor Solution," saying that bringing in international priests is being done for bad reasons. He wrote that in many dioceses it has been "the short-term solution of choice" for the priest shortage. McBrien noted that until recently the importation of priests from other countries had received little or no attention, but the arrival of new priests in Chicago has changed that. He questioned how priests from other cultures will be able to serve the pastoral needs of American Catholics. "Will they understand the changing roles of women and of lay people in the church? How will they relate to American youth?" Furthermore, many countries from which we are getting priests "are in far greater need of priests than we are." What are the motivations of many of the international priests? Are they coming just to get a guaranteed income and standard of living that far exceeds those of their own countries? Do the laity accept them? Finally, McBrien voiced his main argument:

> The most fundamental question of all, however, concerns the nature of the priesthood itself. Is the priest nothing more than a dispenser of sacraments? If so, it really doesn't make any difference whether he is culturally and pastorally attuned to America or not. But if the priest is more than a dispenser of sacraments, this short-term solution is likely to make matters worse, not better.

The column provoked strong reactions. A Nigerian Missionary of St. Paul, Father Cosmas OkeChukwu-Nwosuh, a student at Catholic University, answered McBrien's article with another in the *National Catholic Reporter* on January 9, 1998. He took objection to the word "imported priests." When American and European priests set out to preach the gospel in Africa, Asia, or Latin America, they were called "missionaries," so why should the reverse become "imported goods"? he asked. The term is disrespectful. And why should McBrien insinuate that material gain is the "sole and irresistible motivational factor" for a missionary vocation to the United States? Why should he question the missionary motives of these priests?

Father OkeChukwu-Nwosuh suggested that there is a reason why bringing in priests from other countries had received little attention in America until recently. It was because in the past the priests came from Europe, particularly Ireland, but now they are coming from the southern part of the globe, where the culture is much different. Maybe Americans are objecting to priests of color or priests from developing nations. Maybe Americans are xenophobic, leading them to question whether priests from different cultures are able to function in the American context. In this priest's view, "return missions" from south to north are clearly a sign of the times, and Americans should cherish them. These men may not be from modern nations, but they are from nations where Christianity is vibrant.

In these two articles we see today's debate stated plainly. Should the American Catholic Church continue to invite foreign-born priests? Should it increase the numbers in the future? We have talked with dozens of church leaders and have heard all sides of the arguments. Feelings are strong.

In this chapter we will state the main arguments we have heard for bringing international priests to the United States. Then in chapter 5 we will review the main arguments against doing so.

ARGUMENTS WHY AMERICANS SHOULD CONTINUE BRINGING IN INTERNATIONAL PRIESTS

Two explanatory notes are needed. First, most of the arguments we have heard pertain to bringing in diocesan priests, not priests of missionary religious orders. Religious orders have their own charisms and mission priorities, and in deploying their members they take into account the needs of the world church, not just America. In addition, religious priests make up only a small proportion of the international priests coming to this country. For these reasons religious priests need to be considered separately. Most of what we report below refers to bringing in diocesan priests.

A second note is needed. One argument we occasionally heard will not be included here, since it does not pertain to foreign-born priests serving here for an extended period of time. It states that since the United States has numerous good programs of advanced training, it should invite priests from overseas for training in our universities and seminaries to help world

Catholicism. This argument is valid but outside our scope. Whether or not Americans bring in foreign-born priests for advanced training has little effect on the American church, since those men are here for only a short time.

There are three main arguments for bringing in more international priests. First, America needs them to serve immigrant parishes. Second, we need them to fill in the gaps in our priest shortage. Third, they help universalize and revitalize American Catholicism.

1. America needs immigrant priests to serve immigrant parishes.

Immigration to the United States today is at unprecedented levels, and it is likely to grow even more. Figure 4.1 shows the rates of immigration decade by decade until 2000 and a projection to 2010. The main country from which immigrants came in the last two decades was Mexico. It alone accounted for about 30 percent of legal immigration between 1990 and 2000 (Camarota and McArdle 2003). The next most important sending countries in the 1990s, in order, were the Philippines, Vietnam, the Dominican Republic, and Korea. Undocumented immigrants are in addition to this; the reported numbers of them are no more than estimates, but Mexico is clearly the country from which the most come.

Of all immigrants entering the United States, approximately 42 percent say they are Catholic (Jasso et al. 2003). These people will bring new energy to the American Catholic Church—if they remain Catholic.

The great majority of immigrants settle in only a small part of the United States. The state receiving the most by far is California. After that, in order, are New York, Texas, Florida, New Jersey, and Illinois (Fix and Passel 1994). In general, the regions with the most recent immigrants are also the regions that have the most international priests.

The people we interviewed were unanimous in saying that America needs some foreign priests because of recent immigrants. A former staff member of the United States Conference of Catholic Bishops, now a pastor, said:

> Sometimes the needs in immigrant communities are so great that we have to bring people in to accompany those immigrants. For example, the Korean presence is classic on that. Their priests come to work here for three or five years and then return. Now, the reality is, with them, they can get by without learning English—but it's to their peril *[laugh]* because they can only relate to their own community. They cannot take the role of leader in the community at large. They always have to depend on the laypeople from the parish.

The interviewer asked if American dioceses should incardinate men who are specific to one ethnic group and maybe not so good in English, or if the

Figure 4.1
Immigration to the U.S.: 1820–2010

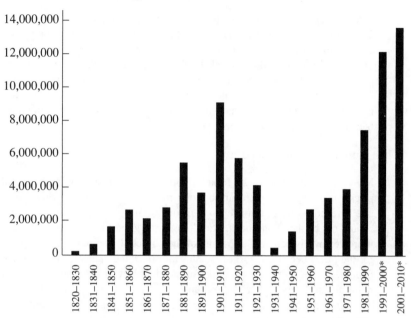

*Projections and graph courtesy *Population Environment Balance,* email uspop@balance.org.

Sources: US Census Bureau; Statistical Yearbook, Immigration and Naturalization Service, www.cairco.org/data/.

dioceses should require that all the men be able to minister to other ethnic groups as well.

> They need to be able to minister to others. It's very rare, at least in our diocese [in California] that a priest would be needed only by one community. And the way our parishes are set up, most of them are multicultural rather than univocal in culture. So a priest, to come in as a young man and to say "I am just going to work in one community," well, you are not going to be very helpful to us.

We asked a priest in Minnesota if he thought the Catholic Church in the United States should bring in more or fewer international priests:

> I think we should plan on having more, because the international face of America is changing. In the Archdiocese of St. Paul and Minneapolis we have the single largest concentration of Hmong immigrants. Also we have a large influx of Samoans. The Spanish population is growing by leaps and bounds. And those are just the few which pop into my head right now. That's the face of who we are here, and our priestly leadership should reflect that face, I believe.

We asked a religious priest in the West about having rules about incardinating international priests who don't speak English:

> It really depends on who you are talking about. I'd say this: in a place like California, if they can serve Hispanics they are more useful than ones who can talk English. So in this context, perhaps, it might be a legitimate idea [to incardinate men who don't speak English]. But I don't think we should be principled on this, because there are too many pastoral contexts that are different. So to make a general rule about that doesn't make any sense, because it binds you to something that you don't necessarily want to be bound to, because there are many different possibilities.

A lay church musician in the East:

> My view is that expecting a broader approach to ministry by international priests is going to be better in the long run. It may be fine to bring someone here primarily to minister to their own immigrant population, but that should not be their sole focus. I don't think it's good for the church because it creates overly separate segments of the church. I also think it's not good for the priest because it sort of isolates him from the mainstream life of the church. And I don't think it's good for the church at large because it doesn't really foster diversity in a healthy sense. If I were a bishop, I would make it a requirement that the foreign priests are here to serve the whole community, not just their ethnic group.

2. America needs immigrant priests to fill in the gaps in its priest shortage.

The number of Catholics in the United States is continually growing, while the number of priests is diminishing. These facts are not in dispute. Figure 4.2 shows the trends. The number of Catholics has been growing at 8 to 12 percent per decade, while the number of priests has been declining at 9 to 11 percent per decade (Hoge and Wenger 2003, 14). Most likely the trends will continue in the future. The availability of priests in the future will be much different than in the recent past.

Is there a shortage of priests in this country? Almost all people say yes. The perception of a shortage began sometime in the 1980s. American Catholic leaders have been discussing and pondering what to do. We authors have experienced program after program for encouraging vocations, including billboard campaigns and radio spots. We have seen postponement of priestly retirement and changed deployment of priests to specifically priestly roles. In spite of all this, the number of vocations and the availability of priests has not increased. On the contrary, ordinations in the United States have gradually declined during the 1990s.

No one should be surprised if some Americans have advocated getting priests from overseas to serve here. A bishop in the Midwest said:

Figure 4.2
Trends in American Catholic Members and Priests

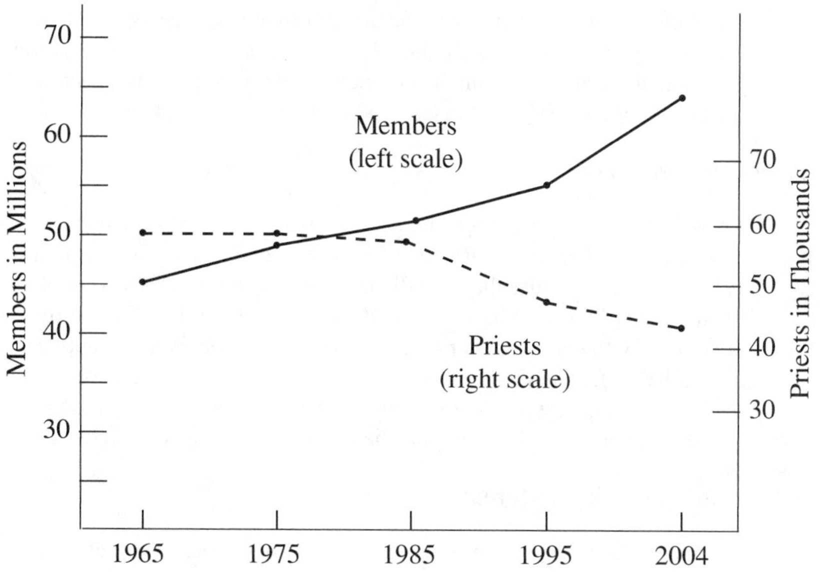

Source: CARA Statistics.

We need to bring in more in the future, not less. We need priests badly, and some areas in the world have them available. If we need to pay for them somehow, okay.

We asked a pastor in the Midwest if the American church should bring in more international priests.

I think we have to! The numbers are dwindling, and we're not keeping up with vocations. I know in Tucson they're importing priests from the Philippines and a lot from Mexico. I just think it has to be. And thanks be to God there are vocations in these other countries, where they have more than they need. So somehow God is working through them. Now *we're* a missionary country *[laugh]*, and they're providing us with missionaries!

He went on to tell of the availability of priests overseas:

I'm not sure about everywhere, but I've visited India twice and visited the bishops over there who had priests here, and talked to them about their numbers and all that. And they were assuring us that they had enough to send us. They had a lot of vocations, and I visited their seminaries, so I didn't feel that we were stealing any of their priests that they needed for their own people. But I don't know about other places.

A vicar for priests in the Midwest:

> There is an excess of priests in some places, like Kerala and Colombia. And
> probably in raw numbers, not too many. But in terms of being able to keep
> them safely employed and un-shot. That's an issue. I see dioceses getting
> more and more engaged with the question of international clergy because of
> the raw numbers. We've got to have them. We need the workers.

A vicar for priests in Texas:

> I have heard directly from men here and elsewhere that the reason those for-
> eign priests are here is because their bishop encouraged them to look to min-
> ister elsewhere, because they just did not need any more priests. That is true
> of Africa and Mexico. I have been told by several of our men from different
> areas of Mexico that the bishops are turning about 50 percent of the applicants
> away. I have often heard the same thing from Africa. They are accepting only
> the best and brightest in a lot of seminaries because the numbers are so much
> greater. So I question the claim that there is a priest shortage everywhere.

A vicar for priests in California:

> There are places in the world that have a far worse priest shortage, and we
> should not be robbing them. On the other hand, there are some places where
> either in one or more countries or one or more dioceses, they currently have
> more priests than they could visibly assign. In my experience, the provin-
> cial of the Philippine Vincentian group that's come here told me that their
> seminary novitiate is full, and they've been ordaining men and they need
> new ministries somewhere. And they could probably have looked for some
> ministries there in the Philippines, but with all of the Filipino immigrants
> who have come here, they wanted to send some here.

A priest who is engaged in acculturating foreign priests:

> I think American priests are conflicted on the issue [whether to bring more
> in], because on the one hand many of them see the need for opening up the
> priesthood. Probably the majority of them do. But on the other hand, they
> are facing day after day specific situations where they've got to have priests!
> "And I don't care where the hell I get them from." Because there are some
> things that aren't going to happen unless you have a priest. The Eucharist is
> going to disappear, and some of the other things. And we *can* get priests! We
> know we can get them!

A seminary professor in the Midwest assured us that bringing in more international priests is inevitable:

> It is inevitable. Look, the Archdiocese of Dubuque, with two hundred parishes,
> lots of small ones of German settlers. Now these parishes are without priests.

There are two hundred parishes in the diocese, and only a hundred have a permanent pastor. Some priests say five Masses over the weekend in five different parishes. Things are going in this direction, and it should be addressed.

Some countries have so many seminarians, it's kind of like Ireland was in the earlier part of the twentieth century. They had so many seminarians they had the freedom to export, and they were happy to do that!

An older priest from India told us of the many vocations there:

Our seminaries are full! My seminary, when I was ordained, had nine hundred students. That's big! I think, when you take the total vocations to the priesthood, India comes in number one or number two in the world. So there are lots of vocations that could be a help to other countries with less vocations.

A priest of the Society of the Divine Word:

The SVD society began in Germany, and it has been mainly European. But now we are getting our vocations from Indonesia. Half of our membership is now from Indonesia. So for us it's just a matter of time till the society will change its character from European to Asian, and it's going in this direction. And this process is going on in the church in general.

The arguments in favor of bringing in foreign-born priests often assume a certain definition of what a priest is, a topic we need to clarify.

A Priest Is a Priest Is a Priest

A traditional slogan is that "a priest is a priest is a priest." Where he comes from, what his training is, what his culture is doesn't matter. This is a plain-talk rendering of the theological principle *ex opere operantis,* meaning that the efficacy of a priest when celebrating sacraments is independent of the spiritual state or the abilities or even the communication skills of the priest himself. A priest, above all else, is an ordained man of holy orders, and he is able to consecrate the bread and wine into the body and blood of Christ. All else is secondary. Advocates of this teaching emphasize the need to have priests available for sacramental ministry, apart from any questions of the personalities or skills of the individual priests. Therefore, bringing in foreign-born priests to the United States is an obvious solution to our shortage of priests.

The vast majority of the people we talked to disagreed with this. They rejected the notion that "a priest is a priest is a priest." For instance, we discussed it with a priest engaged in acculturation programs.

Interviewer: I want to ask about the idea that a priest is a priest is a priest. Who are the people who argue for that?

Priest: I think it refers to the most elementary and rudimentary level of service that a priest provides, in terms of sacraments. It's meeting the first need, and with the vocation shortage and the zero tolerance policy enacted in Dallas, bishops are struggling to fill pulpits and keep parishes open. So the first need is for somebody just to come out and say Mass! Whether he could establish a parish council or set an agenda for a meeting or work collaboratively with laity, especially women, that's so far back in the agenda. Some bishops are really short of men.

A priest who staffs an acculturation program for international priests discussed universalism versus localism in the church:

I think that some of the people have been trained in more classical theology, with a lot of emphasis on the universal church, and "this is canon law, and this is the rule" and that kind of thinking, without attention to culture. There are some international places that stress "we are the Roman Catholic Church, and this is the way it is," so what happens is, the men trained that way come here and they are surprised! Let me give you an example. We had a presentation by a priest who is in charge of gay and lesbian ministry for the diocese, and he was referring to a letter put out by the U.S. bishops to the parents of homosexual persons, and an international priest trained in Rome sees me in the break, and he says something like, "Oh, we covered those things in Rome. Rome is the center of Catholicism. So why are we doing this here?" totally oblivious to the concept that the church has to be the local church, while it also has to be in harmony with the global church.

The priests coming here realize how different the local situation can be. For some of them, as in the case of this guy, who was Korean trained in Rome, what happens, in Rome they're not going to attend to the local Korean situation, and so he finishes his studies there and then let's say he's working here. He thinks, "Well, I'm ready!" But the problem was, what happened in Rome when the kinds of questions about the local church were not raised? So I think it's a conversion point, a point where they start to discover that there is a tremendous longing to be in sync with their own native culture.

Many of the men trained in a mentality of "you are being trained to be a Roman Catholic priest, and we're a universal church, and this is the way it's done all over the world" don't feel the need for local acculturation. [To them] you just come here and this is the Mass, and everything's clear.

A religious sister engaged in acculturation training for priests:

I see cultural diversity as a potential for enrichment, and I think God has revealed God's word with the gifts different cultures bring. So anything less than that is cultural imperialism. We're going to say, "Culture doesn't matter," but what it masks is cultural imperialism. We have to recognize that this is a multicultural world. Essentially a priest is ordained for the Catholic

Church, but each individual priest has his spiritual gifts to bring to the dialogue, and we're all enriched when we share and hear about all the cultures. Having international priests helps us understand the multicultural diversity in world Catholicism.

The majority of the people we interviewed opposed the idea that a priest is a priest is a priest. On the contrary, they said that a priest is a spiritual leader who needs to have the skills, training, and empathy to be able to serve his local people effectively. Nevertheless, the belief that a priest is a priest is a priest is strong in many places in America.

3. International priests help universalize and revitalize American Catholicism.

A third reason for bringing in international priests is their contribution to broadening the vision of American Catholics, so that the laity appreciate that Catholicism is universal, and Catholicism in America is merely one part. Several persons told us that American laity are often narrow-minded, unappreciative of other cultures and languages, and unable to understand the viewpoints of Catholics on other continents. These observers feel that possibly some experiences with good international priests would have an impact on them. American laity, however, usually do not *feel a need* for such broadening, so they will resist pressures to change that do not feel right to them.

Progress will be slow. The possibility of change of this type is present in only a limited number of circumstances. In any case, making it succeed requires having an international priest who has personal qualities of being genuinely pastoral and appealing.

A priest formerly on the staff of the United States Conference of Catholic Bishops:

> It is not the identity of the Catholic Church to just do your own thing locally. We are Catholic, which means "universal," and having priests going back and forth between countries has been a norm since the church began. It's in the spirit of Catholicism to share priests across the continents. So this is not something that is abnormal. Actually it's very normal, and it's always been done. The whole missionary movement has been back and forth. So if you look at it in that light, we need priests here, and there are some places, like Mexico or Poland, where they have more priests than they can use, so let them share them with us. In the past we shared with them, and we sent priests down there. That's the way the church has always operated. Where the need is, you go in and you help out. It's that global thinking that gets you out of being provincial. Not, "We are just going to take care of the American Catholic Church." No. It's universal. Once you take on that outlook, then things have a different take altogether.

We give a lot of money in some of our collections to the foreign missions. But a lot of people here have no idea what is really out there. When you bring in a foreign priest and you get to know him and he talks about his culture, all of a sudden you realize what you are giving [money] for. I think something like that is very helpful and healthy, and that diversity is very good.

A lay diocesan staff person in the East:

I think the American bishops should think and act more globally. We are a very large country, and we seem to be able to live unto ourselves, and in some social justice areas the Conference of Bishops has done well, but I don't find that that filters down to the American people. And I think it's part of our Catholicism to understand that we have a bond and a relationship with all peoples everywhere and that perhaps if we preached and taught more from that perspective and understood that we could learn from each other better, some of the good priests who come here would be more accepted. I find there is a tension these days between bishops wanting to educate their seminarians in a very closed kind of situation near to home, which doesn't help to broaden the vision of the people who are going to become priests. This prevents a greater good which could happen if we had our own future priests educated all over the place.

An international missionary priest serving on the staff of an Eastern diocese argued that the movement of priests should be seen as a training opportunity for everyone:

I think the mindset of a sending bishop from another country should be to ask his priests to come here for a short time, a maximum of ten years or so, to learn as much as they can from the people, from the different structures, the different organizations, the different ministries that maybe they don't have in their own country at this time—to allow these priests to come to experience all that and then go back to enrich their diocese with what they've learned here. *That's* exciting. That thrills me.

You know what would excite me? If the archbishop of New York would send a few men to the diocese I worked in in Borneo for one year. I am sure that would make a *huge difference* to their ministry when they could come back. They would see the whole different value system. The value system of the tribal people over there, it's *very* different. It's person-based. It's spirit-based, with spirituality. It's not just Catholic; it's innate in their culture. To understand the basic human values and the spiritual values of the people there, to bring that back here—the whole idea of the ministry would change. The preaching would change. The ministry to the person would be central. But then again, the whole church needs to change here, too, because the pastors at the moment are so overwhelmed with administration that they can't really be pastors, and that's sad.

A vicar for priests in the South said that he favored having more international priests, even apart from the needs of immigrant parishes or the priest shortage:

> I think a strong reason would be to expose our culture to the universality of our church. Just like I would like to have so many vocations in the United States that we could send our priests to other parts of the world. But many people think more about their own needs than the rest of the world. We live in a world that thinks whatever is around me is what matters! *[laugh]*. But as a church we are constantly reminding people that we are part of a universal church, between our appeals and our teachings. So I see that as a teachable opportunity with the laity.

> I think we need to have a universal effort, seeing that it's not just our need, and we can afford to serve that need, and we have an affluent culture. I think we need to look at the mission of the whole church in the world and to see how we use international clergy in the mission of the church universal rather than how they benefit *us*.

Bringing in an international priest introduces the possibility of breathing new spirit into parish life. The priest may preach differently, teach differently, introduce new music, experiment with new programs, or portray a different spirituality. People recounted to us stories of instances when this happened and how refreshing it was. A veteran American priest said:

> Priests from certain cultures are seen as being more enjoyable to have. The Mexican American culture is very much accepted. The reason is because they are warm and they reach out to people. People love the Vietnamese because they are very industrious and they want to learn, and they really get in there and work at it. So the Vietnamese culture brings in something. And Indians, I heard some very good things about them. Some of them are very pietistic and reverential, and they are good to work with.

A director of an acculturation program:

> Sometimes the joy [of international priests], their simplicity of life, the world that they're coming from, can challenge us in a way that may make us uncomfortable. And I think that's a good uncomfortableness. Another strength is a theology of mission that many of them come with. They come with a real sense of going to do mission work, coming to an area that needs them, and I think that's wonderful and edifying. They come from many cultures where family and religious tradition are very much in the foreground and held sacred. And having them talk about their family or their religious practices, sometimes it hearkens us back to a different age, and maybe we need to ask ourselves, did we lose some of that as a nation and as a church?

A laywoman in the East:

> I certainly think international priests have a lot to bring us because they have
> a worldview that they can give us. When I go to visit my parents on Long
> Island, they have a priest from Sri Lanka who is very good. He brings such
> great thoughts. When he talks about the gospel, he talks about his home in
> Sri Lanka. His words are sweet and very beautiful. I don't know if people
> relate to them, but again, I think the international thing is a good thing.

A veteran lay minister:

> I've worked in parishes for about eighteen years now, and I've worked with
> about eight international priests. My overall view is that all of them that I've
> worked with have been excellent people. Most often they are more than will-
> ing to do any type of project that might come their way. I don't think I've
> ever had one that refused. And they're very good one-on-one. For me, it has
> been a wonderful advantage, because I have learned about new cultures, new
> ways to do things, in some cases a new way to look at some of our things.
> And I think that's true for the parish. One of the priests at the other parish
> brought some music from his country, and it was *incredibly* beautiful! So I
> think we have a lot to learn from them.

A lay seminary professor:

> They [international priests] are sometimes refreshing. The first thing that
> comes to mind is the priest from India, when he entered the church he would
> not have shoes on, because in India when you were in a holy place you would
> not wear shoes. So he would be barefoot. His preaching really spoke to com-
> mon, ordinary, human experiences. There was not a political charge as much
> to his preaching, nor was the preaching particularly culturally charged. But
> sometimes a different perspective. One man used a lot of different perspec-
> tives from Eastern religions.

A diocesan staff member in California talked about the benefits that international priests bring:

> First of all, especially in the Bay Area, there is a large group of immigrant
> people who are being served by men who know them well. It's a great ad-
> vantage for their own people, and I find it to be a great advantage for my-
> self, and I've heard this from a number of Anglos that I know here, that it
> has helped us to learn more about other parts of the world. And it kind of
> stretches us and challenges us to see beyond that which we know or are
> familiar with. It causes me to think about the devotional piece. Have I lost
> some sense of devotion in my own religious life? The international priests
> are better at that because they are so grounded in it. In America the oldest
> guys are that way, and I think the very young are, but the middle-age Ameri-
> can priests, I think, have lost that.

These arguments for bringing in international priests are compelling. America needs these men, and they cannot only give us a world vision but also bless us with their spiritual gifts. We also need to listen to arguments against bringing these priests in; that is the content of chapter 5.

Chapter 5

The Arguments against Bringing in International Priests

> I do think there is a certain band-aid element to bringing them in. I don't think that we need to supply them at all costs, in other words, just for having a warm body to say Mass. *—A lay director of music*

In the last chapter we heard arguments in favor of bringing in international priests. Here we turn to the other side. We heard four arguments for why Americans should stop bringing in international priests. First, there are too many problems with them, mainly in language and culture. Second, bringing priests to America is an irrational deployment of priestly resources in the world. Third, it postpones a much-needed restructuring of parish leadership. And fourth, it postpones lay efforts to recruit more vocations here.

We heard these arguments over and over, and without doubt they are felt widely in the Catholic community. We questioned numerous people as to whether they thought these arguments were strong enough to curtail the flow of international priests to the United States, and the most common judgment was no.

We need to clarify here that American parishioners, on balance, prefer not to have foreign priests serve them in their parishes. They prefer American priests, and the main reasons are language and empathy. Not all Catholics feel this way; some cosmopolitan laypersons felt conflicted and a bit embarrassed when they talked about this, saying that they wished American laity were more receptive to priests from all nations and cultures, but truthfully most laity are not. A real option facing many laity, however, is different, and that is having no priest at all. Due to the priest shortage, many parishes face the choice of an international priest or no priest. In that case they want an international priest.

We turn to the four arguments. The first, that foreign-born priests bring problems, is by far the most common. It has five sub-categories, which need to be explained one by one: language, cultural misunderstandings, different ecclesiology, finances and fundraising, and shyness about mixing with other priests.

1. There are too many problems with international priests.

A. LANGUAGE

Language is the main problem. It came up in all our interviews. It has two distinguishable aspects: that there are priests who never commanded enough English to communicate and that some priests speak English but with such a strong accent that nobody can understand them.

A veteran female lay minister in the East:

> With most of the [international priests] I've dealt with, the biggest block, of course, is language. Parishioners are somewhat taken aback because they can't understand them, particularly from the altar, even though they might be able to understand them one-on-one. It seems that when they get on the altar, it's much more difficult, and that was the case in both parishes I served. I'm not sure longevity helps that. One of the priests, who is still active in ministry, has been in the United States and teaching as well as preaching for over twenty-five years, and it's still difficult to understand him from the altar. One-on-one is not a problem. I have recommended to the priests themselves that they try to get some one-on-one help with English, so that their diction is clearer. I know that's difficult. It's never going to be perfect.

We asked a permanent deacon in the West if priests from any particular culture were especially hard to understand.

> Well, I think Indian priests are difficult, and they're the deepest! They seem to have a rich sense of spirituality, but it *really* is difficult! You have to listen hard. It's just challenging. Today, to articulate with people you really do need people with communication skills. And if we're building fewer churches and have more people in larger churches, it really is paramount that people have those skills. But one-on-one, I think that they're very good.

> If you bring in a foreign priest who cannot speak the language, then you've got a difficulty: you've got people who will not listen. They will come to church and say, "Who's preaching?" I mean, it's pretty human. It's bad enough with just an American priest who's preaching, let alone throw in the culture into it and the language barrier. The people pick and choose. It's no sense in adding to the complexity with a language issue. So that's a concern.

A female eucharistic minister in her sixties:

> I don't like Masses [with foreign priests]. I'm not embarrassed by that. I've
> said this to everybody at church and to the priests. It's just very different!
> It really, really is! It's not just the Hispanic. Our pastor, he's very interest-
> ing. He did missionary work in Central America for a long time. I've spo-
> ken with him about it. I find his speaking difficult. Even though he is from
> Ireland, when he reads a gospel he goes so fast that half of the time I don't
> know what he's saying! It's ridiculous, because he speaks perfect English.
> I've told him before, "Don't go so fast, because you run your words together
> and it's really difficult to understand!"
>
> *Interviewer:* Do you find it off-putting when you can't understand a homily?
> *Eucharistic minister:* Yes. I mean, I would like to see my 25-year-old son
> stay awake. *[laugh].* But his comment is, "I don't understand a word he's
> saying, so I just rest!" And my husband, I notice, will be dozing off and doz-
> ing off. I'm poking him in the side and I'm going, "Wake up, don't do that.
> You can't do that!" But you have to be able to really understand the priest.
> And I wish I wasn't that way, but that's how I feel.

A diocesan staff person from the East:

> Language is a problem. Well, part of the language thing is, I find, an Ameri-
> can problem in terms of these priests' preaching. I find Americans generally
> are very resistant to people whose language they are not familiar with and
> when they have to listen a little bit more carefully to other people preach. I
> find that most of these priests themselves are trying very hard to do well in
> English and to further their English. I've seen them progress along well. So
> it depends on where they come from. It's not much of a problem with priests
> from Ireland or from India. They have an accent, but I find that the problem
> is not theirs, it is Americans who are resistant to making the effort to under-
> stand these priests.

A lay diocesan staff person in California:

> Language is definitely a problem. Overall, people say that they have a hard
> time understanding the accents that the priests have, and the men are not
> clear, especially for the older members of the parishes, who have a hard time
> hearing anyway. They find it extremely difficult and frustrating. So that is a
> definite problem.
>
> I've run into a few men who really have worked hard on learning English
> well and tried to be clear and enunciate well, but on the whole, those I've
> known here in the Bay Area, they resist taking steps to improve their lan-
> guage. Some of the comments I hear are that we are in a world community,
> and people need to learn to understand where *I'm* coming from.

A male Catholic school principal in Chicago:

> The largest number [of international priests] here in Chicago are from India. Indians speak English, but not our English. The parishioners can't understand a damn word they say. My wife and I go downtown to [a particular parish] from time to time. There was an Indian priest there for years. His sermons were well prepared, probably some of the best sermons you have heard during the 1920s! *[laugh].* And you had to strain to get the language. And all the other priests were Indian and really conservative.

A vicar for priests in Texas talked about how well international priests are received:

> I would say that the reception has been very good, with the exception that some have great difficulty understanding some of the Indian priests, in particular, and even some from Africa. And I think our people are not nearly as tolerant of that as they were when the priests came from Ireland, like in the forties and fifties. They spoke English, but you could hardly understand them. And we also had priests not only from Ireland but also from Belgium. So that's been a part of the church in Texas for many, many years. If they're open to working with the people, the people have been very receptive. I currently have a newly ordained guy from Mexico here with me, and this is the largest parish in the diocese and a rather affluent parish. And he's beloved. The people think the world of him. So you can't make a general statement. It depends entirely upon the person himself.

A veteran priest in Chicago:

> Some of the [international] priests are very quiet, because of the language. When they can't speak English, they can be very withdrawn and cautious. Some seem scared, at least at first. If they can't speak English, they feel closed in and afraid. This sets them back.

A Polish religious priest and administrator:

> I think the number one issue is the language—inadequate command of the English language. In most of the places the people have been complaining. They won't tell you in your face that that's the problem, but if you know people well enough in the parish, they will tell you that they struggle with the priests who are coming here because the priests cannot really perform to their expectations. And I think that's across the board. First of all, they don't have a good preparation in Poland. When they come here, they are rushed into the ministry because there's such a tremendous shortage. There's never time to do anything. There's never time for any advanced course. And I think that causes lots of confusion.
>
> If you cannot really communicate with people, how can you minister? You can smile and look good, but if you cannot really get across with the message,

if you cannot minister, if people cannot understand you, it's not good for the people. They have certain expectations. And right now, in the very competitive religious market, you have to provide the best services you can.

B. Cultural misunderstandings

Other problems with international priests were mentioned less frequently than language. The second and third most common have to do with cultural misunderstandings and ecclesiology, and the two are related. In reporting here what we heard, we do not wish to leave the impression that all the American priests and laity were complaining. On the contrary, we heard as many commendations on these topics as complaints. The commendations were usually global ("He's an inspiration"), while the complaints were more specific and diagnostic. Here are examples.

A veteran pastor in California:

> In our diocese we have a large number [of foreign-born priests], maybe half. They would be both from Asia, mainly from Philippines, and Mexico, Central America, and South America. I would say it's been very problematic for our clergy. Some of them don't buy into the church here. This is especially true of the Koreans, who are here for only three years. They come to serve the Koreans here. Most of them did not want to come to the United States, but the bishops sent them. Well, some like it here, but I have seen much more of the idea that "Hey, I am waiting to get out of here" *[laugh]* than they want to stay for a much longer time. Now, some have stayed, have learned English, and have done very well, but their numbers are small.
>
> *Interviewer:* Are the Koreans unique in this way?
> *Priest:* Pretty much. The Vietnamese are all rooted here. The Filipinos usually come to stay.
> *Interviewer:* I have been told of their difficulties with women. What's your experience on that?
> *Priest:* Well, usually it's a matter of accepting a woman, like a woman on the staff, as an equal. I think many of these men come from different countries with a sense of the priest as superior, and that causes a lot of tension.
> *Interviewer:* Is this a matter of priests versus laity, or men versus women?
> *Priest:* It starts with priests versus laity. But also sometimes it's the macho idea, of men kind of superior to the women, and the place of women is to be subservient. Those issues are all out there, sometimes subtle and sometimes blatant.
> *Interviewer:* I am guessing that a woman staff member would be the most threatening.
> *Priest:* Right. She's the lightning rod, because she's there. Usually they have the same degrees the priest has, and they have the experience, sometimes more than the priest has. So, actually, if you were to weigh them on a scale

[laugh] in terms of who is the more effective minister, the women might be the more effective. So that also may be a source of tension.

This priest talked about problems of communication.

Misunderstandings are always there. I think any pastor would feel he did good work if the [international] priest came to him, he said "Hello," had an initial conversation, talked about this and talked about that, he showed him his room and told him dinner was six o'clock. Bang. Now, the guy upstairs is probably thinking, "Gee, I hope he is going to come back and tell me more about it and take my hand and help me." I think there are other kinds of expectations for the people coming in. They might be wanting to enter into a more one-on-one relationship, and so on. I think the priest would say, "I gave him a great welcome," but the other priest would say, "Wait a minute." Or the pastor is thinking, he is an adult man and he knows what to do, he has been a priest before, so he will figure it out. And the guy is in his room waiting for the pastor to tell him what to do. Those kind of things. People have to be told.

We asked a director of an acculturation program for international priests about the biggest problems they have.

I would say misuse of money and women, particularly for the Africans. Just because culturally they look at women very, very differently, and so we have to understand that. But they also have to understand that that is not acceptable in this culture.

Interviewer: When people complain about international priests, what do they mostly say?
Director: It's, we can't understand them when they talk, and they don't understand our culture, particularly when it comes to marriage. Marriage preparation, I think, is very difficult. Particularly for the Indian priests, because some of them might still be coming from seeing arranged marriages, where you don't do any living together or anything like that before marriage. And that's not always the case here. And some of our priests argue that we can't use those priests for marriage preparation until they learn the reality here.
Interviewer: I guess that some international priests would say, "Why should I try to adjust to American reality when I don't even like it, and furthermore it doesn't even conform to what the Catholic Church wants?"
Director: Oh, I know *[loud laugh]*. I've heard that, yes. Or they say "I've come here to save the American Catholic Church, because it's going down the drain!"
Interviewer: Is this a common thing or just a few people?
Director: I know it comes very strongly from the Polish priests. And I've heard it from some of the Indian priests. And some of the African priests are shocked by what they see.
Interviewer: What is the biggest shocker over here?

Director: Many of them would consider us to be kind of free in our sexual mores, like premarital sex and, of course, the whole pro-choice. Some of them find that very, very difficult.

Another priest who works with an acculturation program:

There's some resentment about sort of "Why is it that Father So-and-So, who's from Ireland, didn't have to do this orientation workshop?" You know, most of the priests who get sent to this workshop—I think the color factor plays a role here. They're going to be Latin Americans, African, Filipinos. But if you're someone from Ireland or England, they aren't sent. But they're working in the same diocese. So there's still that prejudice that favors the Northern European. It's assumed they sort of "get it."

Another thing, many of them come from more traditional hierarchical cultures. So when a person of authority, like a bishop, comes, you're always going to wait on them. And when they see a typical middle-class, white community walk out of church and just say, "Hi, Bishop, hi," you know, they're like, "What's going on here?" And so we explain that, well, in the U.S. culture, it's more egalitarian. We don't like titles, we don't like hierarchies, and that's part of the culture. We rebelled against those things. So they'll go, "Oh, oh yeah! So that's why the kids don't stand up when I go into the parochial school classroom. They just say, 'Good morning, Father.' And I thought they were just disrespectful." Or "I thought they were just secular and my priesthood doesn't mean anything to them." So they become more compassionate of their parishioners, of their pastors, and the bishop.

A female diocesan staff member from the Midwest:

There's three priests who come to mind as we talk, who were from India in the highly caste system, and they tended to be in the higher caste. And when they came to working with laypeople, it was much less a mutual sense of laypeople working with the priest to do ministry in the parish. It was a sense of "I tell you, and this is what you need to do." *[laugh]* Which is a very different mode of working, and it can happen even if you're not an international priest. But it came to be even more prominent when it came to gender roles. If they were male lay ministers, they were treated one way, and women lay ministers were treated as another. And those kinds of dynamics happen partly because there was no preparation on either side.

A vicar for priests in the South:

We've had problems with the guys [international priests] regarding women. We've had one case of a guy leaving to get married. But I think that that's just symptomatic of these individuals coming from cultures where they really don't have much association with women. They don't touch women. And then they come here and they're in a parish, and at Mass on Sunday they're hugging, and women are coming up and kissing them. That's a whole new experience for them.

We asked a vicar for priests in California if he has had women coming to him complaining about international priests.

Vicar: Yes. With international priests, it's a pretty big thing, because the rest of the world doesn't see the role of women in the church as we do here.
Interviewer: This implies that the men don't want to hear us say, "This is America. This is how we do things here."
Vicar: They don't want to hear it. Also, they think it's part of the weakness of the American church. So they don't really think it's something that they should be accepting or buying into. They say, "The true church wouldn't be doing this."

The topic of sexual misconduct came up several times. Apparently it is not a widespread problem, but some Americans think it is more common with international priests than with other priests. A vicar in the Midwest talked about priests and women.

Interviewer: Are there problems with the men wanting sexual favors from the women?
Vicar: There has been less of that than I have heard anecdotally from peers, and part of it is, we've created a new transitions program for these fellows, and we address some of that up front, and say, "Here's the cultural pattern you're in. And, by the way, you will go to jail if you do any of the following things."

There is no way for us to know if sexual misconduct is more common among international priests than among American priests, but on basis of all our experiences, we doubt it.

C. DIFFERENT ECCLESIOLOGY

This category of complaint is similar to the one on cultural misunderstandings, but it relates more closely to leadership. A veteran pastor and former staff member of the United States Conference of Catholic Bishops said:

Oftentimes the experiences of most Filipinos and Hispanics is that they come from rural communities where the parishes are much more community-oriented rather than administration-oriented. So that adjustment sometimes doesn't get made. Even though when they work as associates, they keep that community model going, which is very good, when it gets to the administrative work of a parish, often they are not up to it. The problem is most serious when they become pastors of parishes.

Interviewer: I have heard that there may be a latent competition between lay ministers and international priests. Do people ever mention that?

Pastor: Oh yeah. I remember one diocese in Texas. There the previous bishop had lay ministers in different parishes, and the next bishop came in and brought ten priests from India, and *zoom*, they're out. So they feel it.

A priest teaching in acculturation programs talked about an attitude held by some international priests that local cultures are unimportant:

Many of them were trained in a mentality of "You are being trained to be a Roman Catholic priest, and we're a universal church, and this is the way it's done all over the world." So you just come here and this is the Mass and everything's clear. Here are the rules, and you go to it! As long as you have the language down. And if you don't, just work at it.

Interviewer: I'm guessing that a reflective priest would say to himself that saying the Mass in English isn't enough, that he really needs to reach out to the people.
Priest: That's what eventually brings them over to our side. And when we say, "The people will not understand you, because you're not preaching in the language that they understand." And with "language" we mean much more than verbal. So "Unless you learn the culture, you cannot preach the gospel." That's what sells them. There's been some marvelous conversion stories, from people who were resisting.

Earlier I mentioned problems regarding women. A second topic is homosexuality. That's a very, very hot topic! They'll say things like, "Well, that's not a problem. We don't have that in Africa," or "We don't have that in Korea." Homosexuality is something that's not talked about, so they don't have any categories. Someone in his late fifties said, "I never knew there was a difference between orientation and behavior." Something as basic as that, for me, that's frightening. When we talk about homosexuality there'll be resistance from the priests. They'll say things like, "It's these kind of loose bishops who are writing these pastoral letters. Look at what just happened with this priest scandal here in the United States."

We talked with a director of an acculturation program about different ecclesiologies:

Director: One place where I find [differences] is in preaching. The style and the flavor of preaching in the United States are quite different than what they're used to in India or Poland. You know, starting with a story, the familiar reference, the little bit of self-revelation that happens within the context of a sermon or a homily, this is peculiar to the United States and not always present in the countries where the guys come from. I think they need to learn how to preach in the cultural context of the U.S., the same way we would need to learn how to preach if we were in Bogotá, Colombia.

A parish director of religious education:

I had experiences in parishes with priests from Africa and one from India. These priests assumed that there were few roles for the laity and especially as eucharistic ministers, even in one case in the religious education program. And that the women who were directors of religious education shouldn't really be the leaders of those programs, that priests really have to be directors of those programs. So that caused a fair amount of distress on the level of the staff and the eucharistic ministers, readers, altar servers, things like that.

Interviewer: Do you think this would be true of many international priests? *Director:* In my experience it's true in most of the cases. A few, they just sense such a discomfort with that level of involvement on the part of the laity that they stay out of touch with the parish, and they end more as functionaries than pastoral ministers. Not spiritual leaders. But they fill a role, and the older people are still happy to have a priest in that role.

A vicar for priests in the West:

One group [of international priests] maybe come from a culture where the priesthood is the pedestal approach, with lots of hand-kissing or raising the hand to the forehead, and treating them that way. So it becomes very difficult for them to have to participate in parish councils where they are asked to sit and listen, and to welcome the differences of opinions and even critiques. And some have simply an autocratic approach that has them dismiss the people they are serving when they come in with good faith to express their opinions.

A woman diocesan staff member in the West:

There is a distance between some of the priests and the people. So I think that causes a hesitation in relationships. There are some men who, it seems, have become priests here for the better life in America. Especially the Filipino priests. In the Philippines priests are like in a different standard than the rest of the people, so there's a sense of entitlement that they expect, just because they're priests. And that seems to translate across the board to some of the other men that I've witnessed—the Indian men, and some of the Hispanic guys too. And it's definitely more than with American priests. And I think that's a cultural thing, because men in different cultures are, at least in my experience *[laugh]*, they feel they are more *entitled*, whether they are priests or not. And with the Filipino men especially, their families are so thrilled that they've gone to the seminary that it raises them even more. The Irish men I know, I can't say that they feel entitled and are distant. They're more European.

A lay ex-professor in the Midwest:

The majority of the priests in our archdiocese are opposed to bringing in international priests. The reason is that the [international] priests are so conservative theologically that they are difficult to work with. They are rigid, and they preach traditional sexual morality very emphatically. They are strongly opposed to contraception, abortion, premarital sex, and homosexuality, which is alienating for many laity.

D. FINANCES AND FUNDRAISING

A fourth area of complaint against international priests concerns money and fundraising. It is less common than the other complaints, and when it is voiced by Americans, it is done with some ambivalence and nuance. We judge it to be a less serious complaint than the others because of those mixed feelings, as we will illustrate.

A veteran pastor and former staff member of the United States Conference of Catholic Bishops:

> Some [international priests] are coming just to make money. For many of them, a lot of this is family-oriented. In a big family the priest gets the education. His brothers and sisters, unless they immigrate, they are not going to be making any money for the family. If the priest comes to the U.S., he can make money. If he becomes a chaplain, he can make more money, and oftentimes that money is sent back home. It's not necessarily for himself, though sometimes it is.
>
> *Interviewer:* So it doesn't bother you if a man is here to make money, because it is a family project, right?
> *Pastor:* I am not so comfortable with it, but I can understand it. Because everybody has mixed motivations for everything they do. So I can live with a priest who is willing to work hard, and making the money and sending it home. But if somebody is here just for the money, like for himself, that's my objection. There are some cases of that. Not a lot. It kind of gives the other priests a bad name.

A priest from Puerto Rico told us about other Hispanic priests who were raising money in parishes:

> Some priests from Mexico come here on their own to the archdiocese and visit the Hispanic families without any announcement that they will be here. The Hispanic families bring them to their homes. They celebrate Masses in their home, they baptize children in their home, and they take a pack of money back to Mexico. And someone says, "Did you know that Father So-and-so was here, and we gave much money to him, because he's building this golden church in Mexico!" And nobody knows him.
>
> *Interviewer:* So he just came unofficially on his own.
> *Priest:* Yes! And this is a very sad practice!
> *Interviewer:* Is it possible for a man to come in here without permission from his bishop?

Priest: Yes, they do it. I don't know how they do it.

Interviewer: Do you think these men are honest, using the money for the diocese down there, or do they use the money for their families?

Priest: I hope it's for the parishes.

Interviewer: Is this a widespread thing?

Priest: In my ten years here in the States, in almost seven states—because I was a military chaplain—I saw that practice in every state. A priest came to visit some families and stayed.

Interviewer: So they're here raising funds.

Priest: Correct. This is a very, very bad practice! Nobody gave him permission. It's just a private matter.

A priest working with an acculturation program in the West:

I'll give you an example [of finances]. A priest comes from Colombia or wherever, and he is assigned to one parish, but he doesn't mind taking Masses in other parishes or doing baptisms in other places. Well, this guy is moving around in four parishes, taking in fifty dollars for every Mass he says. It's kind of an orientation foreign to the American priests . . . *Plus*, they also go into little businesses for themselves. For instance, they import woolen blankets from Peru, or artworks, or crafts, and they sell it on the side at the local swap meet. I'm giving you a real case that I know of in California. Priests will come here saying, "By the time I leave here, I'm going to have enough money to buy myself a new car." Things like that. Usually these are diocesan priests.

Another priest helping in an acculturation program:

Raising money here for a priest's home parish or home country is frowned upon. But traditional societies always "take care of their people," so therefore the priest is expected to take care of his family. I'm sure a lot of money does pass hands and goes back to the country. Sometimes it goes back to the bishop. Much of the time, I would think, it goes back to the family.

Interviewer: If a man takes money from his own salary, that's considered his private business, right?

Priest: Right. But if he's raising money or asking for money, that's sort of forbidden. But you can't police it very well. It competes with other causes, and it's discouraged. See, the ethnic group would tend to favor the priest and favor his causes privately over what they would support publicly.

Interviewer: Have you run into cases where the foreign priest was here raising money against the will of the pastor?

Priest: [thinks] I do know of alleged cases, but it's not a common thing. But when the priest is having dinner with a family from his country, he'll say he needs something, and they'll give him fifty or a hundred dollars. That's very common.

Interviewer: If a priest is a good friend of the family and says he needs a hundred dollars, would it typically be for his family, or for a project back in El Salvador, or what?

Priest: Probably for his family. Well, sometimes the priest may say it is a project back home, but it's really a family enterprise.

We asked a diocesan staff person in the West if she has seen cases of international priests raising money to send home.

Staff person: Yes. It's done on the side.

Interviewer: So, officially it's not allowed?

Staff person: No. It's not even known—until the people tell you that there's a collection being made. The pastor may not know about it, because they do it on the side.

Interviewer: When they raise money, what is it normally for?

Staff person: Sometimes it's for their home seminary, sometimes it's to re-roof the church back in their home country, sometimes it's for their own personal needs. Just a variety. Our diocese is not clear about the rules. We're naïve. So many times we just trust everything. The person comes in, and we don't think to articulate that there is not to be any fundraising, and if you are to do fundraising, you need permission from the diocese. So they operate under the models of their country. If the priest has sources of income and you can hit the wealthy, then why not? Because they come from poor countries. They think they are doing this for the church in India or in the Philippines or in East Timor or wherever. So I wouldn't fault them totally.

E. International priests don't mix with other priests.

Finally, we mention a topic which came up, but which cannot be considered a major complaint. Rather, it was usually seen as being a situation for which international priests were really not to blame. It was that foreign priests tended to socialize among themselves and not with other priests; thus they often did not become integrated into the presbyterate. Some Americans pointed the finger at foreign priests, some foreign priests did the same at American priests, and many of our interviewees saw it simply as an unavoidable problem.

We asked a laywoman who works with acculturation programs if there is a problem of avoidance:

Yes, there is. I think it's because the foreign-born priests do not really feel they are accepted by the U.S. priests. How many times would a U.S. priest spend his day off with a foreign-born priest? Not many. He will go with his friends, because he feels very comfortable with them. And they'll go and play golf or whatever, which is fine. But I don't think there's that reaching out. And I think the U.S. people are the ones who have to offer it first.

We discussed loneliness felt by some international priests. A lay diocesan staff person:

> Yes, it is a problem! Sometimes it occurs when there is no community for them to relate to. Or sometimes it's that they have not bonded a friendship with the American priests. They don't feel supported. Now, we have eight or nine Indian priests, so they get together, and their support system is among themselves, which is good! But if you have only one Haitian priest or one Tongan priest, where will he go? He will go to the families. Unless there is a real mentorship going on in our diocese towards these priests, there's no way they feel totally in!

We asked a lay diocesan staff member in the Midwest if the international priests feel very welcome here.

> It's probably about fifty-fifty, from the experience I've had. The ones who have said, "Yes, I feel very honored to be part of this place, and they have embraced me," have been those who came well prepared. And there was a place of welcome when they initially came, and work by both the parish community and the priest to understand one another in a deeper way. But for several it has felt like a very hostile environment here, and it probably has been. People see it as if they are getting a second-rate priest. It's "They are bringing somebody in from the outside because we don't have enough members here, and we're not important enough to get an Anglo priest." Which, unfortunately, is still part of the bias.

A priest with years of experience working with international priests:

> We need to find ways in which those priests can connect with the existing clergy, that they can sense themselves as part of the presbyterate in a way that the same kind of respect is given to them, and encouragement and welcome in the rectories, and a sense of belonging. That doesn't always work out, and it's quite difficult. You have to be intentional about it. You have to figure out ways.
>
> Some priests are good about it. The Filipinos all get together and play basketball every Thursday, and they have a big dinner and all that. And the Vietnamese, their people take care of them.
>
> Sometimes it is the fault of the international priests as well. When a priest comes into the rectory, there are certain kinds of established procedures. One would be like dinner in the evening. And I think most pastors would expect that the priest would be in for dinner *at least* once a week, and maybe up to three times a week. But oftentimes that doesn't happen. Like, the Filipino priests are invited out *a lot*. The people love the priests. But that means that the connection in the rectory gets lost, because that's really the time when the priests are together in an informal way where they can be brothers

to each other and kind of get to know each other in a less business kind of way. So when that happens, then the people have to figure out other ways to build relationships with each other, and sometimes it doesn't happen.

2. *Bringing in priests is an irrational deployment of world priestly resources.*

In chapter 3 we introduced the challenge by Philip Jenkins to world Catholicism, saying that the flow of priests to Europe and North America from Asia, Africa, and Latin America was totally irrational in the face of Catholicism's need for priests in the developing nations. The continents with the greatest Catholic growth are precisely the areas that are exporting priests to non-growth parts of the globe. According to Jenkins, even a dullard would know that the church should do the opposite—deploy its manpower in ways that promise the most growth in the future.

We heard this argument over and over. A director of an acculturation program for priests:

> Cardinal Tomko wrote a letter about recruiting priests from developing countries that are much worse off than we are in the ratio of priests to people. It was in 2001. He raises this point, that we are taking from countries that are much worse off than ourselves. And I think as a nation we need to ask ourselves, have we moved this whole consumeristic notion into our ecclesiology and our theology of church? I think we have. The notion that we could purchase vendors from outside to meet our needs. Since we have the money, we can just buy what we want.

A parish director of religious education in the South:

> I think having international priests is kind of indicative of an American mentality. We are five percent of the world's population, and we use thirty percent of their resources. I don't know what those figures are exactly. It's kind of like we are doing it again in the church in America. It doesn't matter if we don't have priests. *Somebody* has them, so let's go use theirs!

A lay diocesan staff member in the Midwest:

> When somebody here talks about the priest shortage, I always think about people in Central America, where they're lucky if they see a priest once every six months in some regions! Is it more fair to be bringing priests from other parts of the world just so we can have Mass with a priest every Sunday? If we're going to redistribute priests because of a priest shortage, let's look at the whole globe and distribute them so all of the people in the Roman Catholic communion are served appropriately. Practically *[laugh]* I don't think it's going to happen in the near future, because so many have a myopic sense of taking care of the local church. Also, it's who has the resources to bring them in!

A priest leading acculturation programs reminded us of financial factors:

> The thing to remember is the social stratification of the more traditional cultures. They have many priests in the cities, enough to take care of the people, but out in the villages and the countryside the people are not taken care of. They have Mass once a year or twice a year or whatever, and that is seen as normal. And yet we ask those bishops to send their city priests over here to take care of our people.

> Historically, priests are distributed according to the possibilities of finances. That's the bottom line. For instance, in colonial Latin America, where were all the priests? They were all in the urban centers; that's where the wealth was. So as a general rule, the priests are going to be where there's enough wealth to sustain a group of professional people who have a relatively distinguished level of education, compared with the rest of the people around them. They won't be out in the boondocks or the hinterland. It may sound rather crass to put it that way, but that's a principle that the church has to acknowledge.

> Now, there are missionary orders like the Jesuits and others that came into existence precisely to work against that idea—to see that there would be a way to fund these men so they could go out to the very poor and difficult places. But that's a principle precisely of the missionary orders and not of the diocesan priests in the history of the church.

3. It postpones a much-needed restructuring of parish leadership.

When we talked with priests and laity about the long-term future, we heard again and again a view that the current priest shortage requires a broader vision of future parish life.

A parish director of religious education in the East:

> I think that a certain number of foreign-born priests will be an asset to this church, but primarily I would like the American Catholic Church to look at empowering laity for more administrative and pastoral roles. I think that's where we should really concentrate most of our energy and effort.

> *Interviewer:* Do you think bringing in international priests sort of postpones that agenda?
> *DRE:* Yes I do.
> *Interviewer:* How widespread is that attitude? I have heard it several times.
> *DRE:* I talk about it among my colleagues, both lay and professed sisters and brothers, and there is some sympathy among that level. I'd be careful about saying that to a priest. I would be particularly careful about saying that to my pastor, because it could mean my removal from my job. Especially in the Northeast, where the institutional church has a very hierarchical model. Our bishop is very definitely a pyramid-type guy in his model of the church.

I think looking at foreign priests as an answer to our problem is not the way I'd want to go. I would look to having our native-born American priests serving liturgically and pastorally, and letting some of the administrative management tasks to the hands of the laity. That's a very early church model—first and second century—and I'd like to see it happen again. We have an educated laity. We are quite capable of doing it.

A lay diocesan staff member talked about the priest shortage:

My personal view is, let us look at who are ordained priests. Can we not look at who really has been called to serve the church? There are married men who are members of the community who are already ordained. Bring them back to service of the church as ordained men! Also there are women who have gifts and have a call and have a right to that. I say, look at the assembly of believers. Look at them and ask, "Who would you call to the altar, please, in your own community where you are?" Why don't we do that everywhere, rather than repopulating the world in another way? *[laugh]* Do it from the people where they are.

Until that happens, I do not think that it serves everyone very well to bring priests in across national borders. I don't think it does. But I've heard people, "Oh for crying out loud, there's all kinds of priests overseas and in different places, what are we doing, worrying about who's going to say Mass here? Why don't we go get one of them?" I've actually heard that from people when parishes were marked for closing. It's just so discouraging. I don't think we *need to be* in this situation. I think we've lacked vision, we've lacked imagination. My God, we've committed a sin against imagination!

The issue is greater than international priests. The issue is, who are we truly as a church, and what does it mean to be ordained for holy orders, and *who* is ordained for holy orders? I think *that* is a bigger issue even than international priests, and that really needs to be addressed. Sure, as long as we can fill the holes with international priests, then we can put off addressing the larger issues. And then you can *deny* that it's a problem.

A vicar for priests in the Midwest:

Some years ago, shortly after our current archbishop came in here, he signaled that he was going to be supportive of our using foreign-born priests. There was some mostly ideological discussion among the priests, where some of our more progressive guys would say, "We've got to kind of squeeze the church on this whole celibacy thing. And bringing in second class fill-ins doesn't let the pain get as clearly felt as it should be."

A laywoman in her seventies said that American dioceses should not continue to import international priests:

To be brutally frank, I think the Catholic Church in America needs to get its act together on a lot of different levels. I think importing priests, just to have a priest at a parish, is not the answer. I know a lot of bishops are going through tough times right now, but the reality is, you might need to close parishes!

A priest on the staff of an Eastern diocese talked about whether the American church should continue to bring in priests:

It depends on why they want to bring in more and more. If it's for the lack of priests here, then no, I wouldn't do that, if it's just sort of like a stop-gap. I think the church here needs to see that they need to supply their own needs. . . . I think we're missing the whole point. We need to rethink the whole priest thing. I know the bishops' conference in Washington is doing a whole consultation on the ecclesial ministry. I think the findings of those consultations need to be made public.

Interviewer: Do you think that the policy of bringing in international priests impedes that process of rethinking ecclesiology?
Priest: It would, if the main reason is just to fill the gaps, yes. We are just holding up the whole process of lay ecclesial ministry and not allowing it to blossom. We're just prolonging what really needs to be done. But if we bring these international priests in to help in the upbuilding of the church, I think that's a great thing.

A vicar for priests in the Midwest:

I think ultimately bringing in international priests is a stalling tactic. It's a stalling tactic because the church is going to have to come to terms with the discipline of mandatory celibacy, over against making the sacraments available for people. And we're not having good conversation about that. This kind of discussion is very, very widespread among our priests—actually among priests who are forty and over and who've been ordained twenty years and over. Some of the newer guys coming in seem to be the opposite: they tend to be more conservative and more obedient to all the practices of the church, and they see them as unchangeable.

A vicar for priests in the Southwest:

I'm not sure that the bringing in of international priests is the solution to our problem. I think we've got a lot of planning and things to do internally. I think we're beginning to look at the whole question of what do priests really do, or what should they be doing in terms of ministry things and who else can participate in those ministries besides clergy. I think the diaconate is a whole area that hasn't been tapped to the extent that it could be. And I think we have to look at the whole vocation issue as a church in this country. My own feeling is, if you have to continue to bring people from other places in as a missionary, it doesn't say much about the strength and quality of the faith of the local community.

4. It postpones lay efforts to recruit more vocations.

An argument we heard from a few priests and one bishop was that if the American church brings in numerous international priests, the laity will relax their efforts to produce their own vocations. Then the laity will feel well served by priests, and thus will feel no pressure to find more vocations.

A bishop from the Midwest:

> People prefer American priests over foreign priests, but we simply don't have enough American vocations. We simply have to get them from somewhere else. But I believe that importing foreign priests makes people relax about encouraging vocations from their own sons. They think that the problem can be solved by importing foreign priests, hence they don't encourage vocations from their own parishes. I believe this is true, and I know that some other bishops believe it too. People have to take responsibility for the priest shortage. There are vocations out there if we nourish them.

A vicar for priests from California:

> As long as people think that they can go out of the country to bring men in, I wonder what we are doing in terms of vocations here. As long as the people in the parishes see the priests coming in from outside, less and less are they seeing it as something their own family can be part of, because if the clergy becomes totally foreign-born, then there's going to be no impetus to have homegrown vocations. If three-quarters of the priests that you ever see are from other countries, you start believing that priests *do* grow on trees.

A lay diocesan staff member in the West:

> I think we have enough men of different cultures in the States right now who are from the cultures that live here, and there are enough families in the States who have sons—say, a Filipino family or a Mexican family or an African family—families who particularly want to have a Mexican or a Filipino or an African man serve them. They should pray and encourage their children to become priests, rather than keep importing them. I just think importing is not the answer.

We heard diverse viewpoints. American laity are slow in welcoming international priests because of experiences with the priests' unusual English and different culture. A few laity also ask, "Why do we Americans have to bring in foreigners, even some from developing nations, to lead us, when we have good Catholic people here who could do it?" And, "Are we being fair in our dealings with poor nations?" These issues need to be taken seriously.

Chapter 6

Motivations for Coming to America

> Many of these people come over to this country to better themselves. But
> when we went out to missions in those foreign countries, you didn't go out
> to better yourself, in fact, just the opposite. You were giving up everything to
> go out.   *—An older American priest*

In chapter 3 we explored the global brain drain and asked if it explained
the movement of priests from country to country. Our conclusion was that
the motivation behind the brain drain in other professions is also present to
some extent in the priesthood. Priests in developing nations have, in general,
a motivation to move to the wealthy, developed nations, since life opportunities, further training, and salaries are better here. Our interviews and focus
groups confirmed this expectation; in fact, there are thousands of priests in
the developing world who would like to come to America. They want this
even though the act of moving to another country can be stressful.

Priests want to come to America. In reality, American bishops have no
need to go out recruiting. We know that several bishops have visited Mexico
or Colombia or Poland to invite priests. But this is uncommon. Most often
we heard the opposite, that dioceses in the United States receive constant
communications from priests in the developing nations wanting to come.

A vicar for priests in northern California:

> I do believe that at one stage my fax, my e-mail, and my phone number were
> written on the walls of every Third World rectory. They were calling me all
> the time. Every other day it was "Father wants to come here." The word got
> out. I was sending maybe ten rejection letters every two weeks.

A vicar in the South:

> The priests come to us. I get requests on the Internet, saying I'd like to come
> and work, or by the mail. They write these letters to everybody. Many of
> them want to come for the summer or for a year. Now, I have started a policy

that we don't take anybody that's not going to stay for two years, because if it's just for six months or so, we're not going to buy them a car, and they can't drive. And for us, that makes them almost worthless.

A vicar from New York:

We have an annual meeting of the New York personnel directors, and I don't know of any of them who have [sent out recruiters]. See, the Archdiocese of New York, they are flooded with these fellows, because they come over here in droves to study, then they tend to want to stay on beyond that. It's not just the Archdiocese of New York, but Brooklyn and all the others down in the area.

A vicar for priests in the Southwest:

In all cases [of priests coming in] they contacted us. And I personally began to think there's sort of a network. Once a diocese shows itself to be open to receiving international priests, all of a sudden you begin to get letters from everywhere: "I know So-and-so that is there." So *[laugh]* the word spreads quickly.

The analysis of motivations is not an exact science. Motivations are usually mixed and partly hidden—hidden even from the actor himself. Nobody should expect a precise categorization of motivations, even less an assessment of the strengths of each, since they are too mixed and hidden. The most we can do is to try to discern motivations of priests and bishops from their own words and from the observations of other persons close to them.

For a priest to come to America, he must desire to do so, and his bishop or provincial must give permission. Therefore, in understanding why they come, we need not only to ask why the priests wish to come but also why the bishops or provincials say yes.

In the last few years, and especially after the sex abuse scandal and the September 11, 2001 terrorist attack, the international movement of priests to the United States has been more carefully monitored than ever. All observers reported this. The old days, when free-lance priests could find their way to the U.S. privately and go about looking for places to minister, are no more. We heard mention of occasional priests who recently slipped through the cracks without getting permission, but they are very few and not worth our attention here.

This raises the question of why the bishop or provincial would give any priest permission to come, when, as we saw in chapter 3, most of the world has a worse priest shortage than the United States. Why do they say yes? There are reasons, as we shall see.

On this topic we need more than ever to distinguish between diocesan and religious priests. Diocesan priests make up the vast majority of international priests in America; they have a home diocese in their country (and a few have an adopted diocese here), where they expect to serve for many years. Religious priests are different in that they belong to international orders that deploy their members to one country or another wherever they are needed, often for delimited periods of time. Their "home" is their order, not any geographic diocese, and they move easily from nation to nation. The missionary impulse is stronger among religious priests for the simple reason that many religious orders have foreign missionary work as their charism, that is, their identity.

In addition, religious priests operate under a different financial system. They take a vow of poverty, which means that their personal finances are handled by the order or province, not by themselves. Their salaries are paid to their order or province, and they receive stipends for living expenses. By contrast, diocesan priests receive salaries directly and find it easier to save and spend money as they wish.

Here we need to recognize the uniqueness of religious priests. This is explained by a religious priest from Poland:

> The religious congregations are different. First of all, we are not a part of a diocese, so we have other missions. We have other duties to perform in the Catholic Church, and usually it's to support the missions. Yes, we sometimes staff our parishes in a given country, but our primary focus will be to minister and to move men to other countries and help where there is a need in the church. We're like special troops. We're not concerned or assigned to a certain place or country. Dioceses are different. They have to worry about their own problems. They have to staff the parishes and make sure they have enough priests.

A religious priest from Vietnam:

> The religious orders focus on the needs of the universal church more than the needs of the local church. Therefore some local bishops do not feel very good in having a large number of religious in their dioceses, because the religious can move out of the diocese. By nature, the religious priest is preaching the good news to new people, so they travel a lot.

MOTIVATIONS OF PRIESTS TO COME TO AMERICA

In our interviews we talked at length about why priests come to America, and we identified five main motivations which, we are convinced, are the main ones. The first two are the strongest—the missionary impulse and the desire for economic improvement. First, the missionary impulse has been fundamental in all two thousand years of Christian history, obeying Christ's command to go, teach, and baptize all nations.

A young diocesan priest from Puerto Rico:

> I came to the United States to be a missionary here. You know, the United States is a missionary country. There is no need to go to Africa or to Latin America. America is the biggest missionary land in the world!

> *Interviewer:* I think there are some places in Latin America where there is not an abundance of priests.
>
> *Priest:* Correct. Yeah. Peru is in need, Ecuador is in need, Bolivia is in serious need. But some places have enough, and they would send some here as missionaries.

A priest member of a personnel board in California reflected on the motivations of priests who come:

> Let me start with the most positive. Some people come, thinking they are really going to do a missionary work. Let me contextualize that just a bit. In their own country, they have so many priests that they don't feel that they are really being used enough, and they know that there is a scarcity of priests here in most of the U.S., except back East, so they feel that in coming here they are going to do a service for the church, and this will be a genuine missionary activity.
>
> Some are attracted by other priests who are friends of theirs, who said how much they enjoyed ministry here and encouraged them to do the same thing. Another motivation is that someone feels he has been misunderstood in his diocese and wants to come and get a fresh start. Of course, we are a little bit wary of something like that. But sometimes if we contact the bishop, and we get some sort of recommendation saying that yeah, this person may benefit by a fresh start, then we may consider the person.

A priest from Vietnam mentioned several motivations:

> There may be many reasons that priests are here. When Mr. Marcos was president of the Philippines, many Filipino priests came to this country because they could be persecuted at home. They had to go. Some other priests want to have some adventure. In America you can develop your skills, and that is a new adventure for you. Some other priests think that this is a rich country, so if they come here and work for ten years, they can go back to help their families in the home country.

A veteran pastor in the West:

> Undoubtedly, many of these men see themselves as missionaries. Many are very fine priests that want to accompany the immigrants. Some, by now, think they want to help save the United States from its priests, from what they've heard about priests here. *[laugh]* Many of them are admirable, generally. Generally I would give the immigrant priests good grades.

An older diocesan pastor in the East:

> I suppose when you really look at our own background as Americans having been heavily involved in missionary work, there are a variety of reasons

why people wanted to join the missions. It's even been said of those in the military service, and it was advertised as such: "Join the Navy and see the world." Perhaps there are some priests that are motivated by reasons other than just the work of proclaiming the gospel. While that may be their motive, they also have other motives. Some are certainly and almost obviously here to better themselves socially and economically. I'm sure of that.

One American priest was skeptical of the "missionary impulse" voiced by many international priests serving in the United States. He asked, "Why did they come *here*? If they want to be missionaries, why don't they go to some other nations where they are needed much more, where the priest shortage is really critical?"

The second motivation, a desire for economic improvement, is less noble, even an embarrassing one to many Catholics. Priests are not supposed to be making life decisions based on considerations of money, the good life, or personal advancement. That's not what priesthood is. Priests are supposed to be dedicated to the needs of the church. Yet in reality these factors figure into their life decisions in hidden or open ways. We found it commonplace for priests, American or foreign, to admit that a desire for money and the good life is a motivation for many priests. Yes, they told us, this is not really "priestly."

A majority of international priests try to hide or deny the economic motivation, and a researcher is seldom able in any one case to say definitely that it is present or how strong it is. It sometimes came out indirectly, as when international priests mentioned to us a strong obligation to help support their parents or family members at home—a fruit of extended family structures in much of the world, especially Africa.

Salaries of priests are much higher in the United States than in developing nations. A 2004 nationwide survey of Catholic diocesan priests in this country found that full-time priests receive an average salary (including housing allowance) of $28,800 (Daly 2005). If they live in a rectory, food cost is near zero. Pension payments are provided. For beginning priests the figure is lower, about $20,000 to $24,000. We looked into priestly salaries in Nigeria, India, Tanzania, and the Philippines and found that they range from $150 to $400 per month, or $1,800 to $4,800 annually. Housing and transportation are provided at no cost. This dollar figure could be misleading if we compare it with salaries in the United States, since the purchasing power of local currencies for basic items like foodstuffs is much higher, perhaps twice as high. We calculated that a priest who receives $300 per month in his home country and then comes to the United States can expect a threefold to fourfold salary increase in buying power, on average. In some cases described to us the increase was greater.

This motivation to earn good money works in the opposite direction from the missionary impulse, since the call to missions includes sacrifice of living standards and convenience, while the search for economic gain is precisely the opposite—a search for higher living standards and more convenience. The two are in tension, and everyone is aware of the problem.

A director of an acculturation program:

> You have to look at the priesthood globally. Priests are moving around the world for the same reason that everyone else is moving around the world, mainly for economic reasons. We need to understand what the economic reasons are, because they certainly influence what happens. You ask a Filipino, "Why are you here?" He'll say, "Well, it's because in my little diocese in the Philippines the bishop doesn't have a parish to give me that can support a priest, and not only do I have to support myself, I have to support my parents. So here I am!" In the United States a priest can make enough money to send some back home.

A vicar for priests from California:

> Sometimes when I was on the personnel board, we asked some of the priests who've applied to come here, "Why are you coming here, because in your own country there is a greater priest shortage than there is here?" One of the comments from one of the priests was very honest. He said, "In my country, there is no such thing as health care, there is no such thing as retirement pensions, and there is no such thing as a regular salary for the priests." He said, "I have relatives that I care about. I am trying to support them and help them. There is a financial advantage for me to work here." I suppose it would be comparable to how doctors and nurses come here from Third World countries.

A vicar for priests in the East:

> They come here for different reasons. If there's an arrangement with the diocese, that's different from a priest who realizes that they have plenty of priests at home and wants to come to the U.S. Also, we have students who come and who want to stay. At least some of them stay here for the wrong reason. They get enamored by the culture and the wealth. They get comfortable here, and to go home and deal with all the poverty and all the issues, it's difficult for them. Most of them we wouldn't encourage to stay.

> *Interviewer:* If a man says he would like to be here permanently, what does the bishop do?
> *Vicar:* It depends on the circumstances, the individual, the bishop, and the reason why they are here. There is this one person in the diocese who cannot go home because of the political unrest in his home country. He is doing extremely well here. I guess if he asks to stay and his bishop agreed long-term,

I guess our bishop would say yes. That's not common. A lot depends on how gifted and adaptable they are, and on the financial issue.

A Filipino priest told about his own motivations to come:

I wanted to experience a new environment, a different culture. I intend to stay here if I'm given a chance to be incardinated.

Interviewer: Some priests from overseas send money back to their families or dioceses. Is that a common thing among Filipino priests?
Priest: Yeah. Usually it's to their relatives. And sometimes it's for projects. People write to us, asking donations to start a church, to build a church, to have a seminary formation program. I know a priest who set up a scholarship foundation, but it's only for his family and relatives. They use the interest for their family members.
Interviewer: Do you think we should encourage more of this fundraising, or should we discourage it?
Priest: Well, I think if it helps, it is good. The value of money is bigger there. When you send one dollar abroad, it has more value there. We have good programs in the Philippines, and we have good projects. Sometimes the parish is poor, so they have to look for funds. And in Vatican II they said that the rich churches should help the poor churches.

Two international priests told us that after serving in the United States for ten or more years, they cannot return. By this time they are so acclimated to the American church that they couldn't tolerate working in the church in their home countries. For them there is no going home. In the words of one:

Take my case. It would be very difficult for me to go back and minister in [my country], because of the different way of ministry. I could never be a priest there.

A lay minister in the East:

It worries me that maybe in the Third World, men enter the priesthood and aspire to come here as a way to better themselves materially and not as a means of a true vocation. I know that one young priest who came to us early in his priesthood, in his late twenties, had to be ordered by his bishop to return to India, and he's back here now! He's serving in this country because he's so totally acclimated to American culture that he could no longer exist in the area in which he was asked to serve. They wanted him back because he was from a primitive tribe in the northern part of India. But he couldn't acclimate when he returned there, so his bishop allowed him to come back here. I don't think it was intentional on his part to come here to experience a better material life, but I think once he did, it made it very difficult for him to return home.

An older priest from India came after retirement:

> I was in the teaching profession for thirty years in India, and according to
> the law of the land I needed to retire at fifty-five. I was a government servant
> in the educational system. Part of my family was here, they wanted me here,
> and I came to visit my family here. I approached the _____ Archdiocese
> while I was visiting here, and they said, "Well, your credentials are good.
> We'll give you an opportunity to work here." They helped me get my visa. I
> came on a tourist visa. They gave me all kinds of help to get my permanent
> visa, and then I started working here.

We need to be clear about why a number of international priests don't
want to go back home. Above we implied that it was because life is easier
in a developed country like the United States, but it could also be for a different reason. After serving for ten years in any country, be it rich or poor,
a person begins to think like the native people. He feels more and more
at home in the new country, and often he has acquired a circle of friends
and a support group that he hates to leave behind. It is common that such
a person, a priest or anyone else, prefers to remain there and not to return
home. We have also heard of persons serving overseas who begin to have a
fear of being inadequate back in the home country, and so they resist going
home. Some Americans overseas are daunted by the social changes; for
example, they see the level of consumption by American families, or they
see computers right and left in America and doubt if they are up to learning
computerese. Maybe it's better not to re-enter America. Anyone who has
lived around missionaries, in whatever land, has experienced how they can
sometimes fear going and then fear coming home.

A third motivation, probably mixed up with the desire for better life and
opportunities, is a desire to be with family members who have come to
America. This was mentioned by a lay diocesan staff member in California:

> We need to look at these priests on an individual basis. Sometimes they are
> coming here because of their families. Family is extremely important in their
> culture. So if their parents have immigrated because their sisters and broth-
> ers are here, and because it gives a better opportunity for their families to
> give education to their children and it is better economically for them, then
> I understand why they're here. So sometimes these priests want to come and
> be with their families, and that's valid for me, *very* valid.

A fourth motivation, already mentioned in the interviews, is a desire for
adventure and new experience. It is difficult to distinguish from the other
reasons for coming, but undoubtedly it exists in some admixture or other
for some priests, probably for the younger more than the older. On balance,
we doubt if it could be considered a major motivation.

A fifth motivation for coming to America, one that is embarrassing for some priests to report, is to escape a situation in their home country. As one might expect, information on priests coming for this reason is divulged cautiously and circumspectly at most. Yet we heard it mentioned numerous times, so there must be some truth to it.

A religious priest from Poland:

> On average, whoever comes to America either had some kind of trouble in Poland or doesn't have a good relationship with the bishop, or simply doesn't feel that he can really actively be involved in any kind of ministry in Poland. The bishops agree. Some bishops look for avenues, and some of them will be sending guys to America. So the superiors in Poland should look closely at the quality of people we are sending for the ministry in America. It cannot be just a proving ground where we will send someone and see how he performs. We should be very much concerned with the quality. So this should be the number one issue: look at quality, not quantity, and try to send good people who can actually do something. Some of the priests are working here because they had either some kind of disagreement in the diocese or they couldn't really function, or there was some confusion or trouble, so it was easier for the guy simply to disappear or to minister here.

A priest directing an acculturation program:

> There are many reasons why priests come over here. Some priests come over here to get out of trouble at home, and some bishops want their priests to come over to get out of trouble. Some come over to make money for themselves and their family. Some come because the bishop at home wants them to make money. A few bishops send their best men over to get a look at the American church because they want to help the priests go up in the hierarchy.

A vicar for priests in the Midwest discussed motivations:

> I don't know specifics, but I hear suspicions that some fellows came here just ahead of the posse. That's the bottom of the barrel at the low end. The other end of it, though, is that America is the land of opportunity, and you make it here by self-assertion and so on, and there are a whole lot of cultures where self-assertion is not a positive value.
>
> *Interviewer:* So they might be bugging the bishop too much?
> *Vicar:* They might be bugging him and actually demanding, "Treat me like a human being!" and asking for the kind of things that bishops don't like to do. The bishop might think, "He might be a pain in the neck and I'd rather not have to deal with him, because his expectations of priesthood are too high."

MOTIVATIONS OF BISHOPS AND PROVINCIALS TO PERMIT PRIESTS TO COME

Bishops and provincials can prevent priests from coming to the United States. Why don't they? Don't they need the priests at home? We asked this question in many interviews and learned that the bishops and provincials have three main motivations for giving permission. First, the bishop in a poor area may not have enough money to support every priest. Second, he may send the priest to America to raise funds for his diocese or province. Third, he may want to be rid of an unsuitable or troublemaker priest. Which is the most common of these we do not know. Let us look at each.

First, bishops are obligated to care for their priests financially, and certainly there are circumstances when a bishop will have more priests than the diocese can afford. Then he may be inclined to send a priest, along with his best wishes, to another country. A seminary professor in Nigeria told us that the Nigerian seminaries are inundated by applicants, and all the seminaries are totally full. Each year more men are being ordained than can be placed, so the bishops and provincials happily send some of them overseas.

An American priest involved in acculturation programs explains:

> A bishop, in canon law, has the responsibility to support his priests economically. And there are some bishops who can barely do that, or cannot. And when they can't do it, they have an obligation to provide it, and if the only way is for that priest to emigrate, they have a moral responsibility to allow him to emigrate. I've heard this from Filipino priests. It's not just supporting the man himself, but like in many parts of the Third World, diocesan priests support their families.

A vicar in the South discussed Polish priests in his diocese:

> It's a lot like the Irish of the previous generation—there's so many numbers that they're encouraging them to find other places. So, many of them are coming over here, first, for the experience of doing priestly work, and secondly for the possibility of incardination. The Polish priest in my parish was asked by his bishop to go to Africa, and then later the bishop asked him to consider coming here. His particular diocese has a strong commitment to missionary work around the world.

Second, we found that a number of bishops in poor nations send priests to America as fundraisers. We guess that this is uncommon, yet it occurs. The cases we heard most about involve priests from India, where several bishops have found that sending priests to America works to raise funds. A priest from India, in his fifties, explains:

> Some dioceses in India, I know, will send some priests to do work here. And some bishops ask that "From your salary and what you get, you give

so much a percentage to the diocese." One diocese near here told the priests that they have to send ten percent, or twenty percent, or thirty percent of their salary to the diocese. So I know that. But for me, my bishop did not ask me to send anything, but every year I send, through my mission preaching, a good amount of money. So maybe because of that he's not asking directly.

An older diocesan priest from India tells about Asian priests:

> Sometimes the bishops in our countries send priests as missionaries to get help from wealthy countries. So the men are like spokesmen for the diocese. Not all of them are like that, but most of the time the [ministry] positions have been misused for collecting money.
>
> *Interviewer:* So a bishop from India might send a man to the United States to raise funds for the diocese.
> *Priest:* Yeah, to some extent. You see, if it is a poor country, it is part of our mission, because the option for the poor is always our Christian tradition, always when there is a problem. And the people in the United States are very generous in helping. . . . The people at home, especially the ones who are poor, they always ask us for help. We priests are in a difficult situation. And also the bishops themselves in the home country make appeals for certain projects, for schools, for hospitals, and the rest. And also individual priests raise money for their own particular parish problems. Suppose they are building a school or an orphanage or whatever. Also the bishop will come here. Bishops always come with a project. One saying is that "When the priests come here, they come either with a problem or a project." *[laugh]*

An older diocesan priest from India:

> The bishop asked me this favor that I come to the U.S. I was not happy to come, but in the end, because of his force, I accepted. You see, from my diocese, we already got three more dioceses erected. For evangelization ours is one of the best areas, and we get a lot of vocations. All of our minor seminaries are packed. We get many ordinations every year, so when we get financial support, we can really do wonders there. The bishop earlier had sent three priests here to raise money. And then they didn't want to return, and the bishop gave them permission to be incardinated here. So then the bishop asked me to come, because every year this mission appeal is a big help. Every year we are able to make a big project.

A vicar from the Northeast told of a religious priest who came to America to support his monastery back home:

> Sometimes there's a particular arrangement with an individual priest. In the case I mentioned, of the religious priest from the Congo, he was the prior of

a monastery over there. And, in fact, he probably sends ninety to ninety-nine percent of his money back to the priory, and he makes no bones about it. The reason he wanted to come here was for the financial benefits to the monastery, not to him personally.

A veteran priest and former national official:

I do know from some experiences that some of the priests have come in with the orders that you can minister in the U.S., but you send back so-and-so much money. The bishop tells them. So what they are doing sometimes is raising funds in the parish to support themselves and support their diocese. But this is not common.

A priest from Poland described various arrangements:

Sometimes it's a two-way relationship. The bishop sends Father Whatever to the States, but by signing, they enter a certain agreement with the bishops in America, and in return he might get some financial support.

Interviewer: Is that a common thing, or is it unusual?
Priest: It's rather common.
Interviewer: So there's a payment if the men come here?
Priest: Yes. I know that the common occurrence among the different religious orders—let's say we are sending Father So-and-so to work, for example, in Germany. But in return the province gets a certain salary, which is for the support of our formation system back in Poland.
Interviewer: So for the province there is a financial gain.
Priest: Exactly.

A vicar for priests in the South:

I found out from one of the priests, an Indian diocesan priest, who said that the priests of his diocese send half of their salary back to their bishop, which then helps their bishop to support all kinds of projects at home, and that encourages the bishop to let priests come over here and work. And I guess that's legitimate. I mean, they are very poor over there. They don't have the money to support priests.

A vicar for priests in the Northeast:

We have two priests from India, and each of them is required to send the diocese five hundred dollars a month. And each of them has said that within their own particular diocese, there is a plethora of priests. So they really are kind of looking for places to place their men.

We asked an official of the United States Conference of Catholic Bishops if there are any financial agreements with dioceses in developing nations:

Interviewer: Are there any financial arrangements so that a diocese, say in Africa, sends a few priests, but the Americans have to pay maybe ten thousand dollars a year?

Priest: No, so far I don't see anything like that, although it was mentioned once between bishop conferences and the American conference. There are no financial arrangements so far. But some people come here just to help their diocese. They send money back.

Interviewer: Are they obligated to do that? Is that a deal with the bishop?

Priest: It is under the table. It is not written down, but it is assumed. Even if the bishop does not say it directly, the sent priest understands the message.

In spite of what this official said, some dioceses make financial agreements with bishops in developing nations. For example, Bishop Sullivan, who retired recently from the Diocese of Richmond, struck a deal with a bishop in the Philippines. The Richmond diocese borrowed priests from the Philippine diocese and in turn provided financial support to needy seminarians there (Vegh 2004).

The third motivation for a bishop to send a priest to America is to give the man further training or an experience in the American church, to groom him for leadership in the diocese later. This is a common practice, but it is of limited interest to our research project unless the priest refuses to return home and stays in America for a long period of time. (We are not focusing on international priests who are studying in America for a delimited short time.) A priest in California told why a bishop in a poor developing nation might allow a priest to come here:

> There is this possibility. A priest that a bishop knows is gifted has a sincere desire to learn and to develop himself, and simply cannot do it if he remains in his country. So a good bishop will try even to help him financially or at least write letters so the guy gets help or a scholarship or what-have-you. So there are always priests moving around who are gifted and just want to develop themselves.

A layperson staffing an acculturation program talked about the problem of students not returning home:

> The priest [coming here] has to sign some kind of commitment that he definitely will return. I know one community of brothers—every brother that they send over to the United States for an education, after they got the education they left the community!

Interviewer: So a bishop may send a man and then lose him!

Staff person: That's a possibility, yes. That's why I think bishops are very careful now. In one diocese they require the priest to come back maybe once every two years to re-inculturate. I think bishops are becoming very wise to that.

The fourth motivation for sending a priest is that some bishops are happy to release a man to serve overseas if the man is a cause of trouble. A bishop doing this will need to hide this motivation, since he is obligated to write a letter of recommendation to the receiving bishop in the United States, and in order to write a positive letter he may need to tactfully withhold some details. A priest from Poland told what happens if a bishop wants to be rid of a man:

> It's kind of like they [the bishop and the man] cut a deal. You know how it is. If you want to fire someone, you write a nice letter of recommendation so he can be hired by somebody else. And that happens. Something could happen, maybe not criminal, but, let's say, somebody has a child. It's very difficult to minister in a Polish environment where everything is close and people know everybody's business. And there's too much pressure on that person. So, in that situation, obviously the priest would have to support the child, but in order for him to work in an unknown environment, the bishop probably will remove him and put him someplace else so he can start afresh.

> However, in the recent years and especially here in the States, with so much trouble with the sexual abuse of children and other things, they're very strict about it, so if there's anything in the background of that person, either criminal or otherwise, I think that will be clearly communicated.

A priest staffing an acculturation program:

> One reason [to permit a priest to go] would be, it always was a way in which you can get rid of priests that are a problem to you. Like, why do public school districts recommend some teachers, when they go to others? And then you find out that they're disasters. Why is that? Well, the school district wants to get rid of them. It might be the same here. So there's no question that we would receive some priests from other countries that had that kind of issue. How many they were, I really don't know.

How commonly does it occur that an overseas bishop sends a trouble-maker to America? We asked this question over and over. Everyone agreed that in decades past this occurred, but it is less prevalent today because the American bishops have become more circumspect. Our guess is that the situation is no longer common today.

We encountered a twist on this problem, which occurs in the caste structure in India. A vicar for priests in the South explained:

> One of the big issues in India is still the caste system. And as best I can understand that, it's really more of a tribal system of families, and that's why you can't get out of your caste. But it appears that if a bishop comes in from a different caste, sometimes he's not as friendly to certain caste members who are present in the diocese. And so the tide changes, and some people who were

in favor are now not in favor, and they may want to leave. And the bishop is inclined to let them go. And the appointment of bishops and what caste they are in, especially some of the lower castes who are appointed bishops and they go into a diocese, it's an issue. But also it is, you know, just [the same] as in any diocese. I mean it could happen to me here, for example. A new bishop comes in and he might be very, very traditional. And he sees me and says, "Well, I don't particularly want you as part of my senior staff. You're free to go. If you can find a job working in Washington, D.C., just go."

An officer of the United States Conference of Catholic Bishops:

> I am not sure how many bishops happily release their priests if the priests are really needed in their dioceses. It could be a sacrifice by the dioceses and their priests to serve the needs of some immigrants in America. But otherwise I am not sure how many bishops allow men who are qualified and who are capable to go. To get a priest, they spend a lot of money. They spend a hundred thousand dollars to have a priest, and if a few years after that they let him go to another country, that does not make sense. They release him either because that man does not get along with the bishop or that man is not capable in the local diocese anymore.

When priests, bishops, and provincials from different countries interact, there are mixed motivations and unclear communications. It is inevitable. Everyone needs to minimize mistrust by being as open and understanding as possible. In the next chapter we will listen to feelings of international priests serving in the United States.

Chapter 7

Voices of the International Priests

Overall I have been well received by the diocese. Partly that is because a lot of priests here are from my country. Maybe that has helped. But I still feel lonely.   —*A priest from Ireland*

The American priests have very little experience of what it is to be a foreigner and to be an outsider. Life is very good to them.
                                                          —*A priest from Zambia*

A central purpose of our research was to hear the viewpoints of the international priests. Have they had good experiences in the United States? Do they feel fulfilled and appreciated? What are their suggestions or complaints? We knew that international priests tend to be cautious about stating their feelings, since many feel vulnerable and uncertain of themselves. Asians, especially, we were told, are cautious about expressing their feelings, and from our experience it is true.

This problem frustrates research, since researchers *need to* hear the true feelings of the men. We did the best we could, partly by having focus groups led by an international priest (Aniedi Okure), partly by spending time putting interviewees at ease, and always by promising confidentiality. In the end we sponsored three successful focus groups and carried out twenty interviews in person or by phone. Also we asked other priests who have worked with internationals extensively to help us understand the feelings of internationals.

The interviews were mixed in quality—some good and some poor, with the main problem being limited English. We were not prepared to do interviewing in any other languages. This experience of doing interviews gave us a sample of difficulties some Americans feel when communicating with international priests. Yet a few of the interviews were immensely helpful, because these men had accumulated wide experience in America and gave us their gut reactions. In this chapter we will convey the main feelings we heard.

It is impossible for us to report the percentages of priests who hold these various feelings, since we were unable to do any sampling at this level of communication and since many international priests are cautious. We give our main attention to expressions that help diagnose problems these priests face. We give less space to vague affirmations like "I have been very happy here." The reader should not conclude from this chapter that international priests tend to be unhappy or resentful; if we give more attention to these feelings, it is merely because the priests' concrete stories and feelings will be the most helpful to everyone in planning for a successful future.

International priests who do not speak English and who expect to return to their countries promptly are not included here, first, because we could not talk to them, and second, because most of them see themselves as merely passing through; thus they are not investing themselves in church life here. We give most attention to bilingual priests who aspire to minister for a long time here.

Three themes were the most common. Many felt inadequately oriented, some thought they were underappreciated, and a number told of unequal treatment. The most common theme was that these men felt inadequately oriented for ministry in America. They tended to blame the system or, in some cases, their first pastor. Why couldn't someone have helped them to learn the ropes better and understand the baffling quirks of American life?

A priest in his forties from Argentina:

> I think everyone who leaves home has a tremendous emotional problem that is a kind of pain that you bear whenever there are reunions or gatherings, when you miss your family, your language, your food, whatever. Personally, I suffer a great deal, coming from a small place, very family-oriented, and in a kind of ministry that was nothing to do with administration but was in direct contact with the people. There were a lot of youngsters, a lot of teens and kids, in a very informal way. The priest was everywhere, and the people enjoyed the priest and the priest enjoyed the people. When I came to America, I felt very lonely for a while, and also I had to try to manage my stress from the administrative things. To prepare weddings was very, very stressful for me: six-month preparation, dealing with divorces, papers coming from different countries, sending letters to the chancery, all that. So I would say in general, everyone suffers when they leave their own country.

> In America I had to update my organizational skills tremendously! And then you have the fees—fees for baptism, fees for this and that. And those laypersons who are sensitive and not educated, they think it's baseless. So we need to spend a lot of time explaining why we need little fees for this and that.

> Everything here is in a schedule. Over there it's more improvised. Here everything has to be planned. Also, as a foreigner you know that your voice is always somebody coming from outside. The pastor will say, "That's good in your

country, but here we are in America." That's okay and correct, but emotionally that puts you a little bit down.

A priest in his forties from Ghana:

It has been extremely difficult. When we come into the parish, some priests welcome you and some priests just know you are there.

Interviewer: What have been the main problems you and your fellows have faced?
Priest: First, I would say, is communication with the pastor. At times there is no communication at all. Some foreign priests fail to inquire what is going on, and sometimes it becomes very frustrating for priests because of the lack of communication between priests in the same rectory. Another experience is this one: there is no opportunity for priests to have a common dinner. In my parish, when you are hungry you go and eat, and hardly ever do two priests eat together. There is hardly any relationship.

A young priest from Argentina:

The first years when I came here, when I was doing little things wrong and feeling like I was only seminarian, it was terrible! I don't know how guys persevere. I had nine years of ministry in Argentina, and I had a good experience there, but *nothing*, nothing that I did over there would fit here! You know, the farmers, the processions with the saints, everything was easy. No intellectual challenge there.

A middle-aged Vietnamese priest:

The foreign priests want to be available to the people, but they feel useless. I talk with many Vietnamese priests who are associates, and the pastors say, "I cannot put him on to celebrate the English Mass because he could not give an effective homily, and the people cannot understand, and they would come in to see me and say, 'If you put this priest on to celebrate Mass, we're moving to a different parish!'" Yes, that happens! I have to deal with this a lot, with priests who come to me for spiritual direction. And when these priests go to visit the parishioners, they are not able to carry on a conversation. It might be a barrier because of language or because of way of life. And then they just stay in the parish. They want to be helpful, but they feel useless.

An older Filipino priest:

It was good that my first experience here with my pastor was very good. There was no problem. It depends on the relationship, how you relate to them, how they relate to you. So, with a different organization, different background, different tradition, different culture, some of the problems arise.

Interviewer: Are there difficulties with the American laity that you experienced?

Priest: At first, yes. It was a culture shock with regard to the tradition of the Catholic Church. They're a little bit different from our country, but we have to adjust ourselves to the Catholic life of the church in the United States. So we have a task of reorientation with regard to acculturation.

A Vietnamese priest, aged forty, told how his pastor helps him:

Here the pastor supports me very much, and he wants me to have a fulfilling ministry. So whatever I think I need, I ask him and he supports me. I am talking about personal things, like the language barrier. He told me to take my time, just go to classes, and learn English more. That is one way. The other way, he lets me meet with my Vietnamese priest friends twice a month, just take the time, even though there are meetings in the parish. He says sometimes there is a nourishment on your ethnic side, because I haven't lost my identity, but also gained my identity by going to some of the Vietnamese priest meetings around here.

In a focus group we asked a Polish priest if Polish priests in the diocese ever feel like second-class citizens:

Yes. And this is how it still is. Maybe it's a little better now in this diocese. Before, they would send the foreign-born priest to the worst pastor, and if he survived, fine. And if he didn't survive, they didn't care about him. Some people are still very harsh. The diocese is not organized enough to welcome newcomers. When I came to this country, I didn't have enough English. I didn't understand the culture, so on my own I took two semesters of English and American culture at [a local college]. I believe that every priest coming to this diocese should have a minimum of six months, maybe a year, of classes to introduce those people to traditions, et cetera, but the diocese is not doing this. One priest came from the Philippines a year ago and they put him in [parish] with the worst pastor, and he is very close to a nervous breakdown. If he will survive, I don't know. There are many other priests who will not say there is anything wrong, because if you say there is something wrong, that means there is something wrong with you. That means you are not adapting yourself to the culture. When a priest is coming he feels he is competent, that he can do everything, that he has the knowledge. But no. This is the reality.

I will give you an example. In our culture in Poland, when you celebrate a birthday or whatever, people will come and they will give you presents. Okay, they will give you this present, and you will take your present and you will say nicely, "Thank you." And you put it aside. However, in America, you will take it, open it, and say "Ah! Oh my God! Wonderful! Thank you! Thank you!" This is a big difference. When I came, I didn't know that. So when I received something, I didn't do that. I did as I would do in Poland.

So they said I am not a cultured man, that I am not polite, that I am not appreciative. Where could I have learned this? This is one small problem.

A young priest from Ireland:

The first time we talked about the culture was when they called all the [newly arrived] priests in for a day of introduction—all the people who came last year. We met with the bishop, and there was coffee and cookies, and all the people from the different departments [of the chancery] came in and told us about what they do. It was a lot of introductions. The bishop is planning another day later, all on acculturation issues. At the meeting we were Filipinos, Nigerians, Indians, Mexicans, and Irish. We went around to say what is the difference between ministering in our culture and ministering here. We didn't talk much. And then we went on to the whole thing about integration and how one fits into the diocese, because they said they don't want people who come here and are just on their own.

It's good they have those two meetings, but I don't think that's enough. I think another thing was that people were very surprised about the whole sexual thing. [In my country] this would not be talked about, even though people know that the priest has a girlfriend or even children. This wouldn't come up. Whereas here, this gets talked about all the time. That was a big thing. It wasn't a question of good or bad, it's just that this was very different. And to some extent, people felt that their own culture was better.

The second theme was that the international priests felt unappreciated by Americans—in some cases by other priests, and in other cases by laity. For us it is impossible to know how widespread these feelings are. An example is a Filipino priest in his forties:

Sometimes people here prefer an American or an Hispanic. Especially when I was new. But I think you have to prove yourself, so they know that you are working hard and that you have something to say, that you have your own abilities. Later on they began to accept me, but at the beginning it was really hard. You could feel the bias. It's still there.

Interviewer: Is this a common thing that Filipino priests feel, that they aren't treated fairly?
Priest: Yeah.

Another Filipino priest told about a problem of acceptance by laity:

There are some people who ask "Where is our priest?" And the foreign priest is just standing right there, and it's a black guy. He says, "Hey, I'm a priest." But the people say, "No, *our* kind." So the other kind is not counted. The colored kind is not counted. That's sad. I have experienced that myself.

A mid-career priest from Gambia:

> There is a problem of acceptance. When I was growing up, we had mission-
> aries from Ireland and France and from this country, and we were happy to
> receive them as priests. There was no dichotomy between white and us, be-
> tween one organization and the other. They came in and tried to bring Christ
> to us. We were happy to have priests celebrate Mass for us. They taught us
> that the church was one, fair enough. We read about Vatican II and all of
> that, yes, the church is one. Then we came over here, and instead of being
> missionaries here, we become "imported personnel." We are given names,
> we have accents, they say they can't understand us. I mean, we are just
> treated as misfits, if you like! You discover that instead of being a priest in
> the midst of other priests, instead of feeling free and being accepted, if you
> ask a question, people turn around and say, "Where are you from? You have
> an accent!" These things are demarcations that you don't belong! Whatever
> you do, you are a visitor. You are a stranger. You have an accent. You are
> black. Call it whatever you like, you don't belong.
>
> If you are American, leave America and go to the Philippines or to Nigeria!
> If you go to the Philippines, you will have an accent among the Filipinos. If
> you go to Nigeria, you will have an accent among the Nigerians. This accent
> thing really drives me mad! Because *all of us* have accents! Even if you go to
> California, you will have an accent! *[laugh]* Why is my accent a problem to
> you? I need to have an accent to have my identity, because I have to identify
> with my own people. So, let us not beat this accents stuff too much. Accept
> it, priests! Try to understand him, people!

A middle-aged priest from Ghana:

> In our seminary [in Ghana] they introduced something called missiology,
> which sees the church as a missionary thing. But I don't know if they have it
> here. That might help them to know that we are all missionaries, and we will
> have missionaries coming in, and we have to accept them. There is nothing like
> superiority, inferiority. If they are broad-minded, they will not think like that.
>
> Missiology tells us plainly that when you go to a place, you have to study the
> area, study the culture of the people, and adapt. That is one of the problems
> we have when we come over here. We need to understand the people we are
> working with, and the people we are working with need to understand us. It
> goes both ways, and the blame needs to be on both sides.

A priest from Ghana:

> There needs to be an appreciation for our training. People ask me where I
> did my training. I did it all in Nigeria. Excuse me! There should be an ap-
> preciation for what we did. No matter where. If a man comes to me and says
> he is a Ghanaian, I'm not going to question his training. I'm going to respect

his training. Or if he is a Vietnamese, if he was trained and ordained back home, I'm not going to question his training. I'm going to respect his training. I'm going to see him as a priest; that's how we were taught. We were taught to see a priest as a priest. It doesn't matter where you were trained or if you were trained twenty years ago. If I have that kind of respect for you, I should respect every aspect. Respect has to be on both sides.

There are people now who are going around to the churches to see who is saying what, and I think it's all over the U.S. And we are not used to this, compared to my experience in Africa, where the priest is very high. Nobody would criticize you. But to think that there are people waiting and watching here, and immediately if you say something they will be phoning up the pastor or bishop. So they put sort of a bad tag on you.

A priest from Mexico had good experiences:

The parishioners [Hispanic] really welcomed me here, because I could speak to them in their language. I understand their culture, so they really welcomed me.

Interviewer: Do you feel that same sense of welcome by the priests?
Priest: They welcome me. The only thing is the language barrier. It is difficult to communicate with them. Not just the Spanish-speaking priests, but every priest. I am happy. I have no complaints.

The third theme was a complaint that they were treated unfairly in placements and appointments. For example, an older priest from India:

Here in this diocese in the past, foreign priests have not been made a pastor. Just now that is changing. Before that, none were made a pastor—just the priests of the land. Now, here we are five or six from India, and we are all qualified, like some university teachers and retired teachers, and now they recognize us and have made us pastors. But before, it wasn't that way.

Even though canon law doesn't put a bar on age for being incardinated, certain dioceses have their own law that a person who is admitted to the presbyterate should be of a certain age. For example, only people below fifty-five are given the opportunity to be incardinated. I was here after fifty-five, I applied for it, and I was not given the opportunity. I have already put in thirteen years of service, but I am still an extern priest. I expressed my desire to be incardinated, but it was not given to me. It was a local law. But I get all the benefits. I have the medical care and other kinds of insurance cheap, but not the pension. So that is something that is not equal treatment!

We asked a Polish priest if other Polish priests complain that they haven't been treated fairly:

Yes, there are isolated cases. Like, for instance, a man contacted an American pastor and wanted a Mass in Polish, and the pastor said no, no, no. Eventually the pastor retired, and they got a new pastor who was trained in Poland, and he said yes . . . Another [Polish priest] complained many, many times, "You got to remember that American priests are racist."

An older priest from Colombia:

The politics in the church here are terrible! It's awful! There is tremendous pressure. If you are a Hispanic, you are not complete, but if you have blue eyes and you come from the descendants of Irish or something, that is perfect! When I was newly ordained here, I was assigned to the dumps of the city. There were Latinos there—Puerto Ricans born in the USA. They had a low level of education, a poor condition. I was not really surprised, because I was coming from the Third World, but we came here with some education, good background, good family, and I was shocked when they told me to come to this garbage, just because I am Hispanic. Even though I have the knowledge and consciousness that I am a priest, that I am going to be accepting poverty, still that was a shocking thing. They gave the good parishes to another guy and the bad parishes to us.

A priest from Vietnam in his forties:

Most of the time when [the Vietnamese priests here] get together, we support each other. And sometimes we hear the problems of a priest with an American priest in a parish, and the bishop always favors the American priest more than the Vietnamese priest. We can see that sometimes they discriminate. The bishop likes to side with the American priest if he says he has a problem with a Vietnamese priest. That's normal, because in this culture we are still a minority.

A Polish priest in the Midwest said he hadn't seen any unfairness:

No, I haven't heard international priests say they have been treated unfairly. Maybe, but not here. Maybe in Poland, but I have not seen it here.

Finally, we invited the international priests to comment on what they found good or bad in American society. This provides useful information for Americans, since international priests offer a mirror by which Americans can see themselves from a fresh and wider perspective. They told us they admired the cultural diversity and cultural richness, the personal freedoms, and the many opportunities. At the same time they criticized the weakness of American families, the feeble sense of community, the excessive individualism, and the tendency to spend money with abandon. Here are several expressions, taken from our focus groups.

A priest from Colombia:

> It's too much self-centered, and they forget the aspect of community. Some-
> times the child has TV in his or her own room! This hinders communica-
> tion in the family; it hinders the sense of basic community. To give time to
> build community is difficult in America. Whereas the other culture I have
> experienced, they take more time to serve, to give time to build community.
> American culture is more individualistic.

A priest from Ireland:

> I find that I get annoyed with wealth that they have. The fact that they can
> spend so much on trivial things, this irritates me. While they are generous
> when they are asked, they seem to spend so much on themselves and their
> children. Another thing is wasting stuff. For example, during Christmas
> they spend so much on Christmas decorations, Christmas papers, Christ-
> mas clothes, everything matches. The same for Halloween. The same for
> Thanksgiving. And then all goes out to the trash bin. I keep saying, I wish I
> had some way to put this in a container and send it abroad. I find it very hard
> to accept this. I find it very hard to accept that they spend so much on their
> pets—and these are Christians, even Catholics! They don't question these
> things, and if you say anything, they say, "What's your problem?" They say
> *you* are the one with problems.

The Irish priest may have a point. It is an example of holding up a
mirror for Americans to see themselves. His complaint about how much
Americans spend on their pets was corroborated in an article in *U.S.A.
Today* (Fetterman 2005). The American pet industry has now grown to $34
billion a year in revenue. That includes everything from pet foods and toys
to furniture and paying fees for dog-walkers, special groomers, even pet
therapists. Dog lovers can buy a $4,000 bed with matching dresser or get
plastic surgery on their dogs or a hair-dying job to cover gray hair. There
are expensive, matching doggie beds, dressers, leashes, and traveling bags.
We can sympathize with priests from less wealthy countries when they
observe some American Catholics spending money in this way.

Another topic was American narrow-mindedness.

An Australian priest:

> I think that the American church needs a lot of openness to the world. They
> are very pious in many ways but still have a way to go in terms of understand-
> ing the church of Vatican II. I think that all American priests should go abroad
> for two years at least. There are many English-speaking countries in Africa
> and elsewhere where they could go. Every priest should go abroad. I would
> say the same thing for members of the religious orders. I have seen that many

of them have never left the States, maybe once or twice for summer vacation, but they have not really let themselves experience a different culture. They've never done it, so they don't know what we are going through . . . They don't see the uncomfortableness, the anxiety that priests from abroad have. It's not that they are bad, but it's because they have never been abroad. They have not been where they cannot speak the language or felt they did not know how to use the local phone or things that are proper to that culture.

In this chapter we have tried to convey the feelings we heard from international priests. We depicted the main themes, realizing that we cannot specify the percentage of men who feel each. These sentiments need to be heard.

In the next chapter we return to voices of American priests and laity, talking about how to improve the experiences of the international priests serving here.

Chapter 8

Issues of Screening, Selection, and Training

> If a priest has been trained here, it's much easier. Then he's ten steps ahead.
> —*A diocesan staff member in the West*

Our research has led us to conclude that in the near future, even in spite of the issues and considerations we have noted, the Catholic Church in the United States will be inviting more international priests in the future. The immediate future will see *more,* not *fewer*. This shifts our attention to a practical question: If the church expects more international priests in the future, how can it manage the inflow to bring forth the most salutary outcome for the priests and also for the church? This chapter looks at seven specific aspects of the management question, drawing on our surveys and interviews.

1. Recruiting and Selecting International Priests

In chapter 6 we reported how vicars of priests in American dioceses receive a constant flow of inquiries from international priests who want to minister here. A vicar in the Northeast who gets two or three inquiries a week explains:

> Most of the inquiries that I get, I believe, it's the shotgun approach. You know, the guy sits down and he goes through what would be equivalent to a Kenedy Directory, and he writes the Lord Bishop of sixteen different dioceses. So I don't think they're aimed at [this diocese] at all.

During the interview process we discussed the idea of redefining international priests as *missionaries* traveling back and forth in an ongoing exchange, with priests going from developing nations to wealthy nations and vice versa. This would redefine "missionary" to fit present-day conditions, in which some developing nations experience more Catholic growth and have more vocations than, for example, the United States, and they could send missionaries here. The wealthy nations would need to pay the bills. This two-way traffic would provide rich experiences for priests from all nations and would remind everyone of the universality of the Catholic Church. Apparently several dioceses are re-visioning missionary work something like this. We heard that the Diocese of Camden has started an exchange program with Costa Rica under which two priests come from Costa Rica to Camden, and two men go in the other direction for two years. The idea deserves study.

We turn to a practical question: If plenty of international priests are trying to come here, which ones should Americans invite? How can we select and screen them? This is a major challenge. To help matters, a standard recommendation form has been composed by the United States Conference of Catholic Bishops for use in reporting if the priest is in good standing and if he has gotten into any trouble. The sending bishop needs to fill this out and sign it, and we are led to believe that this is usually done honestly. Also the document *Guidelines for Receiving Pastoral Ministers in the United States,* issued by the United States Conference of Catholic Bishops, is apparently having a beneficial effect.

We discussed this issue with a religious priest from Poland. We asked if things have changed over the years.

> *Priest:* Oh yes, definitely. Definitely. It's much stricter than it used to be. And I think it's better for everybody, better for the people and better for the priests and better for the diocese.
> *Interviewer:* Over how many years would you say this has changed?
> *Priest:* I would say within the past two to three years.

A Vietnamese priest:

> Right now, because of the many scandals, many bishops are very careful when they accept the foreign priests coming to their diocese. They check the background. In the past they didn't check the background. But now because of the many lawsuits they are very careful in accepting foreign priests.

We discussed with a priest on the staff of the United States Conference of Catholic Bishops whether the book of guidelines for introducing international priests is being followed today:

> In the last few years, yes, they are. In the last three years, even for the American priests who want to move from one diocese to another diocese, it is very difficult. They have to check their background and their personal conduct and everything. For the international priests in the last three years, the dioceses follow the guidelines very, very strictly. Too strictly.
>
> *Interviewer:* Why has this changed in the last few years? For a long time it was different.
> *Priest:* Because they did not see many crises until most recently—the child abuse in the church and also 9/11 and talking about homeland security. So

on the one hand now the bishops need more and more priests, but on the other hand they don't want to take any risks on security and on their dioceses. Many bishops say that they will accept the shortage of priests rather than accepting some priests who have problems.

The difficulty of screening is that the candidate, unless he is studying in the United States, is not available for interviews and observation. Priests and bishops who live thousands of miles away in the sending nation may have local agendas or different standards, and communications may be limited. On whom can we rely for screening candidates? It is a problem. A director of an acculturation program:

> The rule of thumb is: There has to be conversation between the two bishops [sending and receiving]. And the conversation should include: Does this person have problems with women, with pedophilia, with money, with alcohol? You know, direct questions have to be answered, not on a piece of paper, because as you can well imagine, when somebody has a little bomb in their diocese, and another diocese wants it, I'm sure they're pretty happy to give it up! *[laugh]* You know, I mean, this is just human! We always say, create a contract. If you bring the person in, bring him in for one year on a trial basis. If the person works out in that year and seems to be adjusted and works with your presbyterate, then extend it for two, three years. Eventually, many of the priests who have come that way have been incardinated.

Are these cautionary steps being taken in most dioceses today? We don't know, but our impression is that actual current practice is looser than this.

A diocesan staff member in California:

> Our present practice is that we're doing [screening], except that it's not uniformly implemented. So some of these guys come from a contact with, let's say, with a Filipino priest. The priest's friend comes and all of the sudden he's here and fills out the application to stay. We don't have a uniform way to process the men who come in.

A vicar for priests in the West:

> We've tried to put in some procedures of screening that we haven't quite implemented successfully yet. We want to be sure that the priest that we are getting is actually the priest that's been corresponding with us! *[laugh]* Sometimes you have great correspondence with somebody, and you actually talk with him on the phone, and you say, "God, his English is really very good," and then later you find out that he is not the one that shows up. So, we are demanding videotapes, even seeing the man preside at Mass on a video, so we really know it's he that we get.

Some priests who are studying here or who come on their own may succeed in receiving an assignment from a diocese with the understanding that the necessary papers will be collected afterward.

A vicar in the South:

> These guys that come into the diocese, once they're assigned, we write to their bishops or to their superiors, we get all the letters that we need to have for sexual abuse and all that, showing that they're in good standing. And so the system comes to bear, and it works pretty well. But the guys that are floating around are the ones that there are many more questions about, and I don't know how to control them.

This same vicar uses a trusted friend from India to screen candidates:

> One of the ways that I've worked on [screening] is that I've got a priest from India who helps me. I find it very hard to screen a foreign priest. I don't know what to look for. I don't know how to interpret the data. So I have an Indian priest here that I trust. He happens to have his doctorate in Rome in missiology. He seems to have a good grasp of what is going on, so I consult with him. And I found that very helpful in evaluating a guy who wants to come and work here.

> With the religious communities, I have a contract with one religious community. And I work with their General, and that affords us a little more control. You know the organization, you know that they have their own rules and regulations. You know the people involved, and that's helpful.

Can Americans trust the recommendations written by the sending bishops? What if the bishop over there is happy to get rid of a troublesome priest? We discussed this with a veteran priest in California.

> *Interviewer:* Would the bishop over there be inclined to send an endorsement letter if he wants to get rid of somebody?
> *Priest:* That's a good question. Sometimes you get an extraordinary letter of recommendation. But the thing is, because of what happened with the clergy sex abuse and the failed leadership, most bishops are really honest about it and will let us know if we've got a problem.
> *Interviewer:* So, in your judgment, it's not a very common thing that a bishop writes a letter and then says to himself, "Good, I want to get rid of that guy."
> *Priest:* No, it's too serious. So I don't find too many doing that.

2. Experiences with Priests from Various Cultures

Can general statements be made about the suitability of priests from specific nations or cultures for service in the United States? We asked this again and again. As a second stab at this topic, we asked repeatedly if the interviewee would prefer an American priest or an international priest in his or her own parish. The people we talked with were often circumspect in their comments, fearing that their remarks about specific nations or cultures might somehow be prejudiced.

From our research we can make two general statements. First, most American priests and laity have a preference for American priests in their parishes. Not everyone voiced a preference, and a number said it depends on other factors—other than whether the priest was American or foreign-born. Several said that Americans would be better because they are easier to relate to and work with. One or two said that as a matter of principle, all national churches in the world should have their own priests and should not be dependent on missionaries or foreign priests from outside. Therefore the United States should not be dependent on outsiders.

The second statement we can make is that European priests would be preferable over other international priests. European priests learn American-style English more quickly and adapt to American life more easily. One person added that Australian priests would present no problem at all.

Cultural distance was the main consideration here. That is, the more different the priest's home culture is from the culture of the American parish to which he is assigned, the more difficulties will ensue. A corollary of this is that the poorer the priest's home country, the more difficulties there will be—in contrast to America's wealth. Also, priests who grew up in rural settings, which are less cosmopolitan in general, will have more difficulties here. Several persons opined that Asians (except for Indians and Filipinos) have the most struggles learning English and thus are at a disadvantage for adapting to life here.

Here are some representative points of view, some of which are probably based on limited experiences. We asked a professional church musician in the East if he could make any statement about priests from different cultures:

> This is what I have been hearing from people. I think [priests from] Africa are mixed. I've heard some really wonderful stories about African priests who have done well, but I probably have heard more about priests who have not. The cultural distance is too great, and also the language. The language distance is too great to communicate effectively. With respect to Latin Americans, I probably have heard more positives than negatives. Of course, a lot of those guys came here to serve their own populations, but as they've stayed on they've become more mainstream in American diocesan life. So I hear lots of positive things about them. I have heard lots of negative things about

guys from Spain. I've heard that they are very conservative and authoritarian. They are difficult to work with in a team.

A veteran priest and former staff member of the United States Conference of Catholic Bishops:

> I would say that Asians and Spanish-speaking are easier and better to work with than Africans, as a rule. The African cultures are dramatically different! The people are more traditional, and they are less educated, as a rule. The priests have a much harder time to adapt here.

A vicar for priests in Texas distinguished two considerations—cultural distance and vibrant Catholicism:

> The international priests I would want to come here are from a place where the faith is strong and they are strong. In terms of cultural affinities, we have shown as a nation [a preference for] Western European people. It is because, not without reason, they will fit in better because culturally the distance between us and them is shorter than, say, people who have grown up in a tribal village in Africa, which some of the priests in our dioceses have done. There the Mass is Sunday afternoon, and if the sun goes down and they are still into it, the Mass goes on. Then they come here and they are supposed to be over in an hour.

Yet this vicar would prefer an Asian or African priest, because Catholicism is more vibrant there than in Europe.

> The Western European church is probably the candidate to receive priests I would be *least* open to, based not on cultural affinity but strength of faith. The church in Western European countries, with some admirable exceptions, is a church which has lost its way. I would not want to bring priests here who could not make the church stronger. Other than that, my feeling is that we are a Catholic Church, open to all. I would not give preference to a man because of a region of the world he came from. I would want to meet him and know him. It would all come down to the individual.

We heard several times that Korean priests are distinctive in that they almost never learn English, and more often than others they tend to return home after a few years. For them the English language is so foreign and formidable that they tend to remain within the Korean immigrant community.

A vicar for priests in California:

> The area we have greatest concern about with international priests is Korea. Our Korean priests, though we have some very good ones, they tend to be much more insular. They tend to be released here for only three or four years.

They tend to not mingle into the presbyterate. They often have enough to do in Korean that they learn very little English.

3. Young Priests or Older Priests?

Is the American church better served by young or old international priests? We asked dozens of priests and laity, and the clear preference was for *young*. The prevailing reason is that young men adapt to American life better and learn English faster. Other reasons are that young men have more energy, they are more willing to try new things, they relate more affirmatively to American women, especially diocesan staff, and they relate better to youth.

It was not unanimous; we got scattered arguments for bringing in older international priests. We were told that old men have had more ministry experience, they are more considerate, and they have accumulated a longer track record, and so with them you know what you are getting. Two priests argued that the *youngest* priests are risky, since they have had no pastoral experience.

A thirty-nine-year-old Polish priest:

> I think my age was perfect. I came when I was thirty-three. I first got experience of five years of ministering in Poland. If the priest came here right after ordination, I don't think it would be a good idea. A little experience is very good.

A priest on the personnel board of his diocese:

> I think that the priests who are in their mid-thirties and older seem to be able to roll with the punches, and they seem to be capable of adjusting. Some of the younger have come from a hothouse type of seminary experience, even to the point of being in the seminary from the age of twelve on. Some of that shows in their immaturity, so they need to be monitored more closely. The younger fellows, sometimes when they are immature and come here, they usually are sacramental priests—they're comfortable in that role—but they are not comfortable being themselves. . . . The seminary experience is really an inhibiting thing. Some were in the seminary from the age of eleven or twelve, and they just didn't have that adolescence, so they have it after they're ordained.

Several people told us they were unenthused by the recent conservative trend among young priests, both international and American. They thought the young priests' insistence on a clear clergy-lay distinction and a by-the-book strictness would introduce too much tension.

A lay staff member in an Eastern diocese:

> I think men who were formed in light of the Second Vatican Council probably have a different ecclesiology, no matter where they are. But men who

have been formed, let's just say, in the last fifteen years, see themselves as "saviors," that is, they know better than anyone else what the truth really is. And not just international priests. The younger guys, they have no sense of collegiality, they have no sense of a theology of sacrament in the midst of the community.

A trend toward traditional ecclesiology among young priests seems to be occurring in several nations. Earlier research in the United States clearly depicted the trend (Hoge and Wenger 2003), and our advisors reported it in other nations as well.

4. Priests Trained Here versus Priests Trained Overseas

Can any general statements be made comparing international priests trained in the United States with those trained in their own countries, in Rome, or in Louvain? Yes. Of all the people we interviewed, the vast majority said that priests trained in the United States are more suitable. Only a few said that it didn't matter, and no one judged that priests trained overseas are better. The preference for U.S.-trained priests is because they are more adapted to American culture and church life, and on average their English is better. Their seminary training is assumed to have been, in effect, an acculturation period. An additional argument was made by one or two persons, namely, that selecting ordained priests trained overseas is risky due to the difficulty of screening applicants; thus U.S.-trained men are assuredly of better quality.

A veteran pastor in the West:

My plan [for priests coming here for the long term] is that you get them when they are in the seminary, send them to the seminary at the local diocese here, and that serves as the acculturation period where they begin to see how we theologize here, what are the ways in which young men are expected to relate to each other, and then when they do their pastoral year, how they are to relate to women in ministry, the laypeople, and so on. And then they are getting the same kind of theological preparation that their contemporaries are getting, the same kind of devotional emphases.

A lay diocesan staff member in the East:

The priests we have brought from, let's say, the Caribbean and put in our own seminary and then ordained them, I find that they adjust far better overall, and I am wondering if we shouldn't try to get people from other countries earlier before they were ordained, and also have them in a cultural situation in seminary with their own people.

Interviewer: How many years would be the minimum?

Staff member: At least four years of major seminary, and understandably with summers in parishes in the diocese where they would be accepted, working for the bishop later.

Interviewer: What happens if somebody already finished seminary and would like to come here?

Staff member: I would only take them in a situation that was large enough that they could be in diocesan ministry in parishes where there were a number of other priests who could really mentor them, not in a parish where there was just one other priest around.

As we saw in chapter 2, the majority of international priests in the United States were not trained in this country. Only 19 percent of the diocesan priests and 23 percent of the religious priests in our survey completed their seminary studies here. The question arises, if U.S.-trained priests are preferable, why aren't these numbers higher? Why don't we train more of the international priests here? Our interviews provided some information. First, it is more expensive for the American church to train the priests here. Seminary training in other countries is much cheaper. A Vietnamese priest cited figures:

It costs a seminarian here over $100,000 to train to be a priest, about $20,000 a year. But in Vietnam it costs $500 or $600 a year! For four years the total is way under $5,000.

This raises a question of fairness, in that when an American diocese incardinates a priest trained overseas at the expense of the overseas diocese, isn't it unjust? The overseas diocese—in most cases much poorer than the American diocese—has trained the man at its expense, yet he serves in America. The people we talked with all agreed that, yes, it is unjust. One man suggested that American dioceses should pay an "incardination fee" to another diocese—either a diocese in the United States or overseas—when it incardinates a priest who was trained there. His suggested figure: $20,000 for an international priest.

Another reason why Americans hesitate to bring overseas seminarians here for training is a high dropout rate. Some of the seminarians become discouraged and drop out. A priest from India told about his experience:

I went to the bishop here, and I was proposing that if he is interested, I can get some good seminarians and let them be trained here, and they can be priests and work here. But he told me that when he discussed this with some other priests, some felt that some seminarians will come and many will drop out on the way, and not many will become priests, so that means too much expense for us. That problem is there, I cannot deny it. Because even though we bring the best character seminarians from there, after coming here, in their life here they see material advantages of this and that, and surely some people may drop their idea and turn to a different life.

We have no figures on numbers, but observers agree that the dropout rate is high, about twice the rate of U.S.-born seminarians.[1] It is a result of the pressures the seminarians feel when they need to adjust not only to American culture but also to the seminary formation regimen. The double dose can be demoralizing. The high dropout rate lends warrant to hesitation by American bishops before they invest in international seminarians studying here.

A third reason why Americans tend to bring in already ordained priests is that the bishops simply cannot wait! They need priests *now,* and they cannot wait four or more years while the seminarians are studying. The haste solves one problem but brings another: the priests brought here hurriedly often suffer from a too-quick orientation.

To our surprise, our interviews elicited some criticisms of seminary training in America. The feelings came more from laypersons than from priests, yet some of the strongest feelings were expressed by priests. The main disapproval is that American seminary training is too isolated, too sheltered, too much set apart from church life. People told us that seminary life is unreal in that the students are treated too royally and too much removed from the reality of parish ministry. One person bewailed that a seminarian she knows was not allowed to continue contact with his female friends from years past! Another asked why seminarians couldn't be trained alongside lay ministers, since they will be working collaboratively with them in the future.

A second criticism was that American seminaries aren't open enough to other cultures. One person told us that many Hispanic students wanted to study theology but could not because of inadequate credentials, incomplete citizenship papers, or unwelcoming seminary faculty. This person asked, why all the barriers?

In our survey we were able to compare the U.S.-trained priests with the overseas-trained to see how different they were. We expected that the U.S.-trained priests would be more adjusted to American society, more acculturated, and more relaxed, but in the survey data the differences turned out to be small. Perhaps the American seminary education did not include enough exposure to American culture. This is a guess; we do not know the true reason.

Our experience in this project alerted us to the strong feelings in the Catholic community today on various topics pertaining to vocations, seminary training, and priesthood. We heard fervent opinions from priests and from laypersons. People at all levels want to have input into the church's future direction.

1. Katarina Schuth, author of *Seminaries, Theologates, and the Future of Church Ministry* (Collegeville, MN: Liturgical Press, 1999), by personal communication.

5. Diocesan versus Religious Priests

We asked our contacts if, in general, diocesan or religious international priests serve the American church better. The majority said religious priests. Quite a few judged that it all depends on the individual, and no general statement can be made. The general preference for religious priests is grounded in several reasons: they receive training more suited to cross-cultural ministry; they are more internationally minded; they have more built-in support groups; and they are less interested in diocesan politics.

A priest involved with acculturation programs:

> Let me speculate a little bit about religious versus diocesan. Religious tend to have more support groups, more support structures, so I find that they're usually not as isolated, and they tend to be not as nervous or defensive, because they've had people walk them through new situations. Also they tend to have more places where they process some of this, so as they're going through culture shock, they've had a chance to discuss it. Just the difference between having dinner with a community at night, for example, versus, if you're a diocesan priest, you're either by yourself or in your room eating. That can make a big difference! Another thing, I think the religious communities often have more of an international sense, especially the ones that are very international. They've crossed cultures before, so a lot of the men have been in other countries, and they bring those skills.

A veteran American priest observed that religious international priests often come with an *esprit de corps* from their order that helps the men make the transition to the new life (Kemper 1999).

A priest working with acculturation programs:

> The religious are better at training men for different cultures. In formation, to have those cultural experiences sets the stage for the priest to know that you just can't move from one culture to the next without adjusting to the new cultural reality.

One priest who worked at the United States Conference of Catholic Bishops brought up a question of control:

> There is a problem I am seeing more and more: many bishops do not want to invite religious to help. One of the reasons is that the religious are not under the authority of the bishop; they are under the authority of the provincials. The bishops think, "You don't really belong to me." Some bishops are open to invite religious to do something, but they don't want to see the religious priests become rebellious, so to avoid the problem they do not invite them.

6. Short-Term versus Long-Term Service

Which serves the Catholic Church in the United States better—long-term international priests ministering here their entire careers or short-term international priests cycling in and out? All agreed: long-term is better. The optimum pattern, from the viewpoint of the church in America, is career-long international priests who can minister to English-speaking Americans as well as their own ethnic group, who psychologically "buy into" American culture and the church in America and who are incardinated. This is the ideal on which everyone agrees.

(A long-term ministry in America does not mean a long-term ministry in a single parish or a single type of ministry; probably some shifting around is better. That question is not our concern here; we are considering only the length of time the priest is serving *in the United States*.)

We were told that four or five years of ministry in the United States should be the minimum, and international priests should be recruited with this as a condition. The reason is that four or five years are needed to improve the priest's English and to learn the subtleties and peculiarities of American life, such as baseball, Halloween, the Superbowl, and the Internet. Most important, it takes several years before a priest can typically become immersed in American culture enough that he can invest himself fully in it and thereby become a pastoral and spiritual leader to his flock, as opposed to merely a sacramental leader. In the early years, even his preaching won't communicate. A lay diocesan staff person in the East stated the consensus view. We asked her if international priests should be expected to stay in this country X number of years minimum.

> *Staff person:* Yes, I do, just as we do with pastors, for a three to six-year period. Anything shorter is really not worth it, because before that they really can't be part of the community. They're still visitors.
> *Interviewer:* Someone has said that pastors who know they are here only for a short time do not really buy in.
> *Staff person:* Yeah. Many people who know they're going home soon will not get as involved. We want people here for the long haul.

A vicar for priests in California:

> My parents live in the Diocese of Honolulu, and their parish is staffed by two international priests that are on five-year commitments. They are good men, both are Filipinos, and they are dedicated. I personally like them. But I get a sense that they really want to go home. And why shouldn't they? Their brothers and sisters and parents are all home. If the place where they're serving is not home or doesn't look like it's going to become home, their investment in terms of what they give and in terms of the way they allow their local church to change *them* is going to be minimal. If you know that you

are a visitor, you are going to be much quieter about what you believe, what you invest in, as opposed to one who is going to stay and who says, "Here is where I'm going to plant myself. I have to give it my all!"

In our discussions we heard repeated arguments that dioceses need to be flexible in matters of short-term or long-term commitments. Several ethnic communities, of which the Koreans are the best known, demand priests who command the Korean language, and these parishes can be provided with priests only through contacts with Korean bishops to supply priests in a five- or six-year rotation, with no expectation that they will learn English. Another condition requiring flexibility is the availability of an older priest whose ministerial career is certain to be short and who will never speak good English; he needs a short contract but no incardination.

Questions of incardination policy come up at this point. Most dioceses prefer incardinating priests who are fluent in English as well as their native language, and a number of dioceses absolutely demand it. Their rationale is that incardination involves a long-term commitment made by the diocese to a priest, and he needs to be versatile, able to minister to as many laity as possible and able to relate to the rest of the presbyterate.

7. Best Assignments for International Priests

Deciding where to place international priests is complex, since all concrete situations are unique. One must consider what is best for the priest and what is best for the people. Close behind, one must consider the overall needs of the diocese. Unavoidably, clerical politics enters in.

With international priests as with newly ordained priests, the first assignment has long-run consequences in the man's ministry. It must be thoughtfully planned. Everyone we spoke with agreed that the first assignment of an international priest must be one in which he will be welcomed and helped. This is the single most important consideration. Being assigned to a pastor who ignores him or has no interest in him invites disaster. An international priest should first be placed as an associate; he should not be put in a parish alone. This is easily said but not always easily done, since numerous dioceses need priests to serve in outlying parishes, where the priest will be alone, and international priests are easily relegated to boondock parishes that the American priests don't want.

Beyond these basic principles on which everyone agreed, our advisors made various suggestions about specifics. Here are some. Several persons said that international priests should be assigned to parishes with well-educated, cosmopolitan parishioners; such parishes will be the most interested, appreciative, and supportive. These parishes will usually be urban or suburban, but not always. Several suggested that the priests should be assigned, if possible, to communities in which some people of their nationality are living, either as parishioners or as other people around town; this will reduce the problem of loneliness.

A middle-aged pastor in the Midwest:

> I think the city is a better place than a rural area, because I think in the city, people are used to hearing different people. You've got more of a mix of people. And I think just adapting to a whole different accent is harder in a rural area. In the city you've got a little more opportunity for them too. We only had one restaurant where I was, and they didn't serve Indian cuisine. [The Indian priest there] would eat Chinese food—he liked Chinese food—but that wasn't served there, at least very often. It was all German-Russian meat and potatoes type of thing. He started cooking himself, and that's how he survived. He learned how to make rice.

A professional church musician in the East voiced a caution:

> My guess would be more cosmopolitan areas would be best, the places with higher educational levels. People need to have appreciation of the priests. But in some way, more traditional parishes could be a better place to live in, whereas in places with higher educational level, it may be that the people will be able to understand their culture, but they would be asking why we need foreign priests and saying that we should ordain women.

Language acquisition is a factor. Do we want to pressure the international priest to learn English quickly? If so, don't place him in a parish with people who predominantly speak his native language, because then he won't practice English. Place him in a multicultural parish where English is demanded of him. One veteran priest said that young international priests, as opposed to older men, should be placed in parishes with few people speaking their native language so that they will acquire English quickly. Older priests are different. Since they will learn English slowly, if ever, they should be put with parishioners who use their native language.

Several vicars and priests told us that African priests often get along poorly with African American parishioners. From other research we know this is a problem not only with Catholic priests but with African immigrants generally. The reasons for the bad feelings are complex, and this is not the place to go into them. Yet the problem is real. Many of the persons we interviewed suggested that priests coming from Africa would be more successful in parishes other than African American parishes.

We received many suggestions about acculturation programs and language training. They are central to our research project, and they will be reviewed in the next chapter.

Chapter 9

Orientation Programs for International Priests

> Nobody briefed us about the situation here or how to function. It was like, "Okay, we'll send you and try to do the best you can. We'll drop you in the water. Try to swim. If you swim, fine. If you don't, you die." That's their approach, and I think it's wrong.
>
> —*A Polish priest in his forties*

Our research has convinced us that international priests need better orientation for ministry in the United States. About 380 to 400 of them are beginning ministry here each year, of whom 30 percent were trained in American seminaries. For the moment we assume that the 30 percent received some orientation to America during seminary, and we turn our attention to the others, the men who came after ordination. What preparation did they get when they came? From our survey it appears that a small percentage got excellent orientation, a larger percentage got a small amount, and the rest got nothing. In this chapter we look at what is needed and what could be done to meet the needs of ordained priests when they come. At the end of the chapter we explore the major acculturation programs in the nation today.

WHAT IS NEEDED?

Our survey, focus groups, and interviews agreed fairly well on the priests' needs. They can be summarized under three headings. First, some of the priests need help with English, either comprehension or speech with an accent that Americans understand. Not everyone needs this, and it is a sensitive matter of judgment as to who does. As we noted in chapter 5, a number of international priests feel that their English is every bit as good as the twang they hear from Americans, and they feel no urge to adjust to the American version of English. Another portion expect to be ministering mainly to their own ethnic group, and for them English training is optional. On average, American laity see English training as more important than the international priests do.

Second is orientation to American culture. This encompasses both a broad understanding—such as information on the American founding fathers, the Civil War, Abraham Lincoln, and Martin Luther King, Jr.—and also concrete information on the problems of everyday life.

Third is creation of bonds with other priests. As we have seen, loneliness and lack of support afflict a large number of international priests. They wish for strengthened bonds with other same-language priests and also stronger ties with American priests in the diocese.

We asked the experts and international priests over and over, What is being done today and what should be done in the future? We look at the three needs in turn.

1. Help with the English Language

Priests lacking fundamental knowledge of English need classroom instruction. Depending on how good their English is when they arrive, this may entail a few months or a year, maybe even full time. A Polish priest told us that priests need *good* English to be real pastoral leaders and spiritual leaders. With minimal English they can say Mass, but this should be seen as a temporary minimal situation, *not at all* adequate for real ministry.

A parish director of religious education:

> If we are going to have a flow of international priests, there ought to be some kind of orientation program which is much like an English as a Second Language program. But it would be broader than just the language; it would be the language and the culture. I am not aware of any of these for priests.

Helping priests who speak English but with an accent unfamiliar to Americans calls for a different program. Our advisors agreed that in that case the priest needs a tutor or speech coach.

A professional church musician had suggestions:

> I would like a person assigned to help the priest with speech communication training who would meet with him afterwards. He would say that "This word has a meaning of . . . ," or "If you could alter it a bit, it would be clearer to people." Priests could also be recording their homily so that they can go back and say, "Oh, I think I should modify that." That's what I would do. This should go on for a year. It's really difficult to change many muscular things that we learn. It takes time. Maybe there is someone in the parish who would volunteer their time or be paid a small stipend to provide the service. Or we might find another priest who would offer that.

A vicar for priests in California told of hiring a company to help the new priests:

Just this week we had an information program about a course in mastering American English that we are going to offer in September. It's by a company that works with business professionals, helping them to improve their pronunciation and reduce their accents so that they could communicate more effectively in their businesses. This group is willing to do this with priests, so we had nine priests sign up for it at the meeting on Monday. We are going to have a second information session in a couple of weeks, and there might be others who will also take the course.

2. Orientation to American Culture

All our advisors agreed that more orientation is needed than is now being offered. They also agreed that orientation needs to take place over a period of time, maybe a year, probably with an initial educational session, then periodic meetings or consultations. Simply having an introductory series of lectures for a few days at the beginning is ineffective because it provides no opportunity for the priest to consult with an advisor later when culture shock hits.

Further, our advisors agreed that orientation should be done as locally as possible. The best location would be in the diocese and even in the parish where the priest is assigned. Small dioceses probably cannot put on orientation programs for their small numbers of international priests, so they should participate in regional programs. Several persons proposed that seminaries should be asked to provide facilities where these programs can meet.

There were two more consensus conclusions. First, the best orientation program would include a mentor or a person designated to accompany the new priest for a period of time. The mentor should be publicly announced so that everyone knows who he is and so that the international priest feels totally free to make use of him. The mentorship should continue for at least a year. Finally, a good orientation involves not only the international priest but also the receiving parish and its pastor.

Aside from these areas of consensus, we heard many reports of what is being done and many ideas of what should be done. Here is an example. A young Polish priest spoke approvingly of a program in which he participated in the Archdiocese of Chicago:

> We had three sessions of acculturation. They were in the seminary at Mundelein, and I think they were very helpful. There were different speakers. They talked about the diocese, and we could learn about the history of our diocese. It was a good opportunity. The first session was a three-day meeting, and we stayed there overnight. One day we went to the Pastoral Center, and we had a half-day trip to Catholic Charities. It was not only for Polish-speaking extern priests.
>
> *Interviewer:* Is this required for all extern priests, or is it optional?
> *Priest:* It was optional.

> *Interviewer:* Are most priests interested in this type of program or not?
> *Priest:* I can say yes, most are.

Another Polish priest made suggestions for orientation programs:

> I think that they should have a crash course first in Poland or whatever the country of origin. Number two, they should have something here, either inter-diocesan, let's say with several dioceses together developing a program and some training, or each diocese should have its own. But I think if they could unify and have several big dioceses working together to develop a program, it would probably be easier to organize, develop, and staff. If I were a superior, I would make it a requirement, without "ifs" and "buts." All priests would have to do it.

> *Interviewer:* Can you tell me why it doesn't happen now?
> *Priest:* Most of the time when you [come here and] hit the ground, you get right to work because there's such a tremendous need. They don't want you to go and "waste your time" quote-unquote, on something else. They want you to go and work in parish A or B. But I think that this is not good planning and not good thinking. They should first prepare the people the best they can so they can function best in the parish or other religious environment. If somebody who comes speaks good English, has a good understanding of the culture, and knows how the church is different than in their country of origin, that person will do better than someone who comes off the boat without any preparation and tries to bring his own ideas from the country of origin and tries to implement them in America, because that won't work.

A vicar for priests in the Midwest talked about his diocese's house of transition:

> The priests move into the house as soon as they come, so they get a place to live when they get here, and they're in the house a minimum of two months, depending on their English skills. They may be in longer if they're in a more intense language-study program. During that time they go out and do some weekend work. Mostly they're in English class or accent management class. And we bring in guest speakers with them who talk about everything from driving in America to boundaries issues. It's a real mix of things.

> *Interviewer:* Are there priests who don't want to do it, who say, "Aw shucks, I've already been a priest. Why do I have to go through this silly stuff?"
> *Vicar:* Most of them are very pleased, because they find the States pretty intimidating. And there's pretty good P.R. for the program among the international clergy themselves, so they become its best advocate.
> *Interviewer:* Is there anything after the man leaves?
> *Vicar:* We continue to bring the international clergy together, although for the most part, what we're trying to do then is to integrate them into the normal fraternal life of the diocese. I just hosted a dinner at my house a few

weeks ago for the Spanish-speaking fellows, and we're doing another one in two weeks. We're trying to get a monthly thing going. No big agenda other than "Hey, how are you doing?" It was well received the first time. We'll see if it picks up enough steam to become self-sustaining.

A parish religious education director in the East:

An acculturation program should be *required*. It should be staffed by people running diocesan offices and people who actually work in parishes. I think there should be some classes in American popular culture. They should meet with parish liturgists and parish priests. I just think they should be given some kind of immersion course in what parish life is like by meeting a lot of people from parishes. I think it would take two or three months. It should be at a diocesan seminary or something like that, but *in the diocese*. Every diocese is going to have its own culture, so if you're going to work in a specific culture, what's the point of preparing in Texas and then ending up in New York?

A vicar for priests in the East:

To me an attractive program would be *within the diocese itself,* so that a person has the experience of a diocesan community while they are learning what they are experiencing. It's almost like a CPE-type program, where they are going often to the parish and they get feedback, and a supervised ministry program. I would combine the two. It would be a superb idea.

Interviewer: Why don't they do it?
Vicar: There are so many things to do. *[laugh]* And because of the shortage of the priests, you have the priests having all kinds of extra jobs. The personnel director is a pastor of a parish, the continuing ed director is a pastor of a parish, the vicar for clergy is a pastor of a parish. So they are stretching everyone. A lot of these extra things which could be very helpful are put kind of at the bottom of the list.

A Vietnamese priest talked about the obligations of the pastor:

Don't just put the men into the parish, where the pastor doesn't know much about them. That makes it miserable to all parties—the pastors, the parishioners, and the priests coming in. The pastor presumes that these guys have a driver's license, know how to drive a car, know how to cope, how to do laundry, how to do this and that. For example, a guy from Africa. There the priest is viewed like a king, and people take care of him and his needs. But if you put him in a parish here, he will say, "What's going on here?" *[laugh]* So the pastor needs to help these men, orient them, and show them that they are useful, not useless, so when they come in, both parties can help each other and appreciate each other, rather than pointing the finger and saying, "What you do in your own culture does not fit here, and you are not effective here." The priests don't know the situation here.

Several people listed topics that should be included in orientation. The topics include driving, driver's training, cooking for oneself, etiquette—such as using a knife, fork, and spoon—hygiene, including the necessity to bathe daily, street slang, street language, shopping without haggling, dealing with the post office and government offices, computers, medical and dental care, and credit cards. The rules and problems of rectory living need to be covered. One person suggested some travel within the United States, if there is enough money.

Several people elaborated on the need for an accompanying person in the first year.

A director of an acculturation program:

> It could be the pastor, or it could be another cleric. But somebody who really knows what it's like to do the priestly work here in the United States and understands the cultural differences, and to really walk with them as they're going through it. For example, one of the parochial vicars at the parish in the beginning, he would meet with the person maybe every other day, just to kind of sit down and talk. "How have these last two days been for you? What has been challenging for you? Where have you felt empowered? What can we do to assist? What do you feel is missing?" And then this person would give the new priest some feedback, like "I noticed that you talked very quickly during your homily today. It might be better to pause and to speak more distinctly." That kind of thing. And also companionship. Just going out with them, taking them out, say, they go out for a day off. What happens usually is they're left home while the U.S. priests are taking their days off with their friends.
>
> *Interviewer:* This implies that the accompanying person has to have some pastoral skills.
> *Director:* That's right. And he also needs to know what the reality is that the person's going through.

A director of an acculturation program:

> It can't be that you just show them around for a weekend and then you leave them alone, because there's constant things going on: banking, credit cards, how do I manage the accounts of the parish, how do I get a car, how do I get insurance? I think there needs to be somebody in the diocese, either the vicar for clergy or one of the auxiliary bishops, somebody assigned to international priests, who can attend to this question of hospitality. The priests need to be assigned a mentor, not just somebody that they happen to find informally. It has to be intentional, and they have to be assigned somebody for the first year at least. When our own guys get ordained here, many dioceses across the United States assign them a mentor or ask them to get a mentor, and it's an intentional relationship that helps them in the initial years of priesthood. Why is it any different with the international guy coming to the United States?

A young lay minister told about an international priest at his church:

> I am concerned about [international priests] getting mentoring once they begin. A good example was the first priest from Africa at my parish. People were complaining about his homilies, and the priests there weren't willing to talk to him about his homilies, because priests don't talk to each other about their homilies. And these are good guys, but they were afraid to say something to the guy because they didn't want to hurt his feelings or whatever, and let him die out there every Sunday, versus buying him a cup of coffee and sitting down and talking to him about it.

A Midwest diocese has an elderly Indian priest who takes responsibility for orienting the incoming priests. The vicar for priests explains:

> He or myself will meet the priest that comes over for the first time. And he'll take him to his parish for about two weeks. During that time he'll read with him to practice English and help him prepare a sermon, and just make him feel more welcome and more at home. In the meantime he gets the man his social security card and almost purchases a car for him. And this priest is very willing to help in that area. I have a problem with all of the INS papers, but [the Indian priest] is good at it.

3. Strengthening Bonds with Other Priests

Priests need bonds with other people from their home country, and they need bonds with American priests.

A parish lay minister:

> I would be cautious about where I sent [the international priests]. I would try to send them to a place where there would be some natural community for them, amongst fellow priests or even people from their country. And I would put a lot of emphasis on mentoring them once they are here. I think the guys that I've met who haven't done well often seem to be awfully isolated without much support.

A priest helping in acculturation programs:

> Presbyterates need to think in terms of very practical things. Most diocesan priests have family in the area, and while they're young, their parents are living. So on their day off they can go to their brother's home or their sister's home, see the family, take a nap, have dinner, and spend the day with their family. What do international priests do on their day off? One of them told me, he said, when we all get together on a Thursday and do something socially, the other priests complain because all the Indian guys are going to do something. They complain because they see us as being cliquish. But none

of them have invited us to their homes, none of them have asked us to do those other things. None of us have families here in this country.

A priest in his forties from the Philippines:

> In the Philippines they have a program for the newly ordained priests for five years. They meet together at least once a month and then share their experiences. And somebody is taking care of them; a priest is assigned to them. So I think a program like that for priests would be good.
>
> *Interviewer:* I suppose the archdiocese here does not have that.
> *Priest:* No, no. Here you are on your own. You do your own thing. Well, we have recollection, we have retreats and meetings. But it's still lacking. In the Philippines, I was a parish priest there for sixteen years, and in our diocese we have a sports festival for all the priests of the diocese. We have teams of priests, and we play. Also we have cooperative banks where the priests put in money and you can borrow. The cooperative in our diocese is really big. I think they have maybe one hundred million, and you can borrow enough to buy a car. Yeah! Right now we have that! Because of that the priests know each other. They see each other in other places, so there is camaraderie.
>
> I think we can set up a program here for new priests, maybe a one-year or two-year program for orientation at first and then maybe monthly meetings for a year. And recollections. Because it's really hard. I for one experienced this. I almost wanted to go home! Because you're alone; you have nobody until you find Filipino parishioners. But they are too busy in the United States. They work so hard!

A lay church musician in the East:

> We need to help them develop relationships and friendships, you know, the normal human kind of interactions that will nourish them, that are really important. I can't help but think how isolated a lot of these guys feel at times in the communities where people don't really "get" *[laugh]* who they are and what their background is. I think the priests are probably going to need the skills to begin to make those connections happen. That's part of the ongoing help that I think they need. I think we should bring in international priests in groups and put them where some of their nationality are there already.

An international priest serving as a staff member of the United States Conference of Catholic Bishops suggested restructuring:

> We need to be more flexible in using priests. Why must a priest stay in one parish? Why don't we have some centers? We could have four or five priests at one center, and that center can work in ten different parishes. Instead of being my own boss, we can have a group of people sharing experiences together, having community life, even with diocesan priests. They can share

problems, they can support each other, and they can learn from each other. So instead of fighting against problems in that parish by himself alone, he can say something to other people who have the same problems and who are expert in some other situation. If we can restructure, the shortage of priests will not be a big problem.

ORIENTATION MUST INCLUDE PASTORS AND PARISHIONERS

We were told repeatedly that orientation programs must involve more people than just the international priests themselves.

A lay diocesan staff member in the Midwest:

> International priests as they are currently being brought into the country are not necessarily being brought into a situation that's healthy or hopeful for them or the communities here. There needs to be preparation for the priests as well as the parish communities and the civic communities, to welcome them in a way that allows them to flourish. If we're going to continue to bring in international priests, which I think is a natural piece of being a global church, then we do need to spend time and energy on providing the best possible situation for that to happen.

A parish director of religious education in the East:

> I think before a priest is stationed in a parish, the pastor should make announcements for maybe three or four weeks and talk about welcoming the priest. And I think once the priest arrives, there should be social mixers after each of the Masses for a number of weeks, where he gets to meet and greet people over coffee and cake, so that people really feel like they know him. Now we just put them in the parish and assign them Masses and assign them baptisms, weddings, and confession schedules, and we don't do anything on *our* part to help them integrate.

A director of an acculturation program said that several persons in the parish need to be part of the welcoming process:

> I would say that the accompanying person and even some other members of the parish, like the parish council president, maybe the musician in the parish, and the secretary—anybody who's interfacing with the new priest—needs to go through a preparation because, hopefully, there's going to be a transformation on the part of both groups—the individual coming into the parish and the parish and its members. They're all going to be changed by this process.

RESISTANCE AND OBSTACLES

International priests who have gone through orientation programs almost always praise them, as we have seen, raising the question of why these programs haven't been developed more fully by now. What is holding them back? Don't bishops and priests see their value? Our research has shown that many bishops and American priests today are not convinced of their value, or at least convinced that the value is worth the cost. In some other cases it is a matter of priorities: the diocesan leadership feels overwhelmed and unable to do anything more. We have also heard of situations where the diocesan leadership needs the priest so urgently that there is no time for any orientation.

There is another barrier. Some of the international priests themselves do not want to attend orientation programs for whatever reason, and diocesan leaders are loathe to pressure them. Even if the program is required by the diocese, the rule often cannot be enforced if pastors or international priests refuse. One director of acculturation programs made an observation:

> I think one reason is, if a bishop required it, it might deter some men, who might then go to another diocese. And I think the programs have to be crafted in such a way that they build on the experience of the men coming in. It can't be "seminary take-two," because that's insulting.

A veteran priest in California:

> The [international] priests may refuse to attend an orientation program. They might think they are priests and have had enough experience.
>
> *Interviewer:* Is it a common thing?
> *Priest:* I don't know how common it is. Judging from the number of priests who *don't* apply for these programs, there are many. They don't want to.
> *Interviewer:* What if you say, "Father, this is not for my benefit, it's for *your* benefit."
> *Priest:* Or, better, "Father, if you don't go, you are not coming to the diocese."

A priest involved in acculturation programs speculated that they might be seen as needed only by men having problems:

> I think that sometimes it's seen as a punishment. Like, "Father is really not doing well; he doesn't get it; the people don't understand him; he's rude; he's offensive. Let's send him to this program."

The same priest speculated that most bishops don't perceive the importance of training in cultural differences:

> I think most bishops are still operating out of this idea, "Well, they're Catholic priests, and I'm sending them to Catholic parishes, so okay, the only thing is if

their language is right." I'm not convinced that they are really convinced that the priests have to be more versed in intercultural dynamics.

Another American priest:

> They [the pastors] support orientation programs in name, but not if there's any other pressure. They're very pressed for time and money, so if they've got a funeral coming up or they've got regular Masses, the pastor is more apt to insist that those things get done rather than say, "We won't have Mass today, we'll just have a Communion service, and you go ahead to the program."

A priest on an archdiocesan staff in the East discussed both orientation and support systems:

> I think it needs to be organized. The bishop would have to give it some standing, and it would have to come from, say, the priest personnel office, so that it tells the person coming in that the archdiocese is really interested in his welfare, it really wants to look after his interests, to listen to his concerns, to help explain to him some of the things that he will face, and also to listen to him about what his culture can bring. I think *that* part is often missed—that he knows he is heard, that he is understood, that he is bringing something into this country and not just providing a service.

MAJOR ORIENTATION PROGRAMS TODAY

We learned that not everyone is acquainted with the major orientation programs available today. Several people told us that there are no programs out there or that there are none in their part of the country. They are uninformed. We heard of six or eight programs underway in various places, and we talked with the directors of six of them. All are happy to become better known. Here we give basic information on them.

1. COPIM—Cultural Orientation Program for International Ministers

Begun in 1990, this program was sponsored by the bishops of California for international priests ministering in California and part of Nevada. The co-directors have been Rev. Kenneth McGuire, C.S.P., and Rev. Allan Deck, S.J. The standard program entails three gatherings of two and a half days each, spaced throughout one academic year. Its main emphasis is on understanding cultural dynamics and how to minister to the local American culture.

Contact information: Cultural Orientation Program for International Ministers, Loyola Marymount University, 1 LMU Drive, Los Angeles, CA 90045-2659. Phone: 310-338-2799. Website: extension.lmu.edu/religion/COPIM.

2. The Southeast Pastoral Institute Program

The Southeast Pastoral Institute (SEPI) was created by the National Conference of Catholic Bishops in the 1970s to serve the Hispanic population in nine southeastern states. The director is Rev. Mario Vizcaino, a Piarist priest. It has an orientation program for priests from Latin America. The priests live at SEPI's office in a dormitory in Miami and take classes and language instruction. Some stay a week or two, others a month or longer. SEPI has no fixed program; everything is tailored to the needs of each individual.

Contact information: Southeast Pastoral Institute, 7700 S.W. 56th Street, Miami, FL 33155. E-mail: sepimiami@aol.com. Phone: 305-279-2333.

3. Maryknoll's Cross-Cultural Services Program

The Maryknoll Fathers and Brothers, at their headquarters north of New York City, have been orienting international priests since 1997. The program offers a five-day workshop, which can be run either at the Maryknoll headquarters or in a diocese. The director is Sister Kathryn Pierce, I.H.M.

The program's main emphasis is on assisting the priests in adjusting to their new environment as well as to understand the acculturation process. The Cross-Cultural Services prefers priests to come only after they have been in the Unites States for a couple of months.

Contact information: Maryknoll Cross-Cultural Services Acculturation Workshop, Box 305, Maryknoll, NY 10545. Website: www.maryknoll .org/ccs. Phone: 914-941-7636.

4. Institute for Black Catholic Studies

The I.B.C.S. at Xavier University in New Orleans offers a three-week intensive program every summer on ministerial leadership in the American black community. It welcomes international priests, sisters, and laity who will minister in the United States. Most of the international students are from Africa or the Caribbean, but American students also attend. The subject matter is Catholic theology from a black perspective. The director is Sister Jamie Phelps, O.P.

Contact information: Institute for Black Cultural Studies, Xavier University, 1 Drexel Drive, Box 49, New Orleans, LA 70125. Website: www.xula .edu/ibcs. Phone: 504-520-7691.

5. Vincentian Center for Church and Society, St. John's University

For five years the Center has sponsored a five-day acculturation seminar at St. John's University on Long Island, designed for international priests who have been in the United States for at least six months. Teachers are university faculty, local pastors, and foreign-born resident priests. The emphasis is on understanding the church in the United States, American culture, communications, and the acculturation process. The director is Sister Margaret J. Kelly, D.C.

Contact information: Vincentian Center for Church and Society, St. John's University, 8000 Utopia Parkway, Queens, NY 11439. Phone: 718-990-1612. Website: http://vincenter.org. E-mail: VCCS@stjohns.edu.

6. International Priest Internship, San Antonio, Texas

The Oblate School of Theology in San Antonio, Texas, received a foundation grant for a five-year experiment to develop an innovative acculturation program. In spring 2005 it was in its second year. The director is Rev. John Kemper, S.S.

The priests come for three weeks in the summer for an introductory session on the American culture and church, then return in January and May. Each priest is given a laptop computer for use during the year. The program is open to priests in every diocese in America.

Contact information: International Priest Internship, Oblate School of Theology, 285 Oblate Drive, San Antonio, TX 78216. Phone: 210-341-1366. Website: www.ost.edu.

For more information contact the Committee on Pastoral Care of Migrants and Refugees, United States Council of Catholic Bishops, 3211 4th Street, N.E., Washington, DC 20017. The director is Rev. Anthony Dao, O.P. Phone: 202-541-3357. E-mail: adao@usccb.org.

Chapter 10

Conclusions and Recommendations

We began this study by asking broad questions about international priests serving in the United States. How are they faring? Are they ministering effectively? Should the church in the United States continue to bring them in? What should be done to aid them? We carried out surveys, focus groups, and interviews, and, as the earlier chapters have shown, the interviews with vicars for priests, American priests, and American lay leaders turned out to be the most instructive. We have quoted from those interviews time and again. All this research has led us to a few conclusions and has produced several main recommendations.

First some conclusions. We have seen that the church in the United States has had a long history of bringing in international priests. The flow of missionaries to the United States began in the 1800s and grew until the 1940s and 1950s, when it abated. Over the years this nation has brought in many more missionaries than it has sent out. Only in the 1940s and 1950s was the opposite the case. Today Catholics with a short memory often think that the United States, being such a wealthy nation with such a strong Catholic Church, has always sent missionaries abroad and should be doing so now. They wonder why international priests are here, and they are not receptive enough to the idea. These persons are operating with a mythical, not a factual, past.

The long history of bringing in priests has had mixed success. From the start there were tensions over ecclesiological and cultural issues, since European priests in the nineteenth century preferred a more hierarchical church and saw little merit in the separation of church and state. American bishops complained about the quality of priests sent over from Europe. Now, a century later, the complaints are again the same, but this time they are about international priests from Africa, Asia, and Latin America, whose culture is much different from that of most Americans. Again Americans complain about language problems and cultural misunderstandings.

The situation today is so similar to that in the early twentieth century, and what is said about the African and Asian priests is so similar to what was said then about the Europeans that the greater cultural difference today between the origins of the priests and American culture do not seem to be so crucial. With either large or small cultural distances between incoming priests and laity, the complaints have been similar, making us wonder how important the more distant origins of today's international priests really are. Maybe the mentality of American priests and laity, exhibiting pride that America is different and somehow ahead of the rest of the world, is the most telling factor, and the specific origins of today's international priests less so. In any case, we are certain that given the variations in the characteristics of incoming priests, many of the complaints are justified.

What has clearly changed is that the international priests today are more visible and more exotic. They stand out. Also what has changed is that the priests come from developing nations that are now experiencing rapid Catholic growth—nations poor economically but, from one perspective, rich spiritually. Americans today take pride in their national wealth and leadership, and as a result wonder, often subconsciously, if Africans or Asians really have anything worthwhile to say to them. This is a subtle ethnocentricity that irritates priests from the developing world. The international priests, in turn, take pride in the Catholic growth in their homelands and subconsciously feel they have a deeper spirituality. American Catholics need to see Catholicism in world terms, and they need to learn about their own past. They need to discern what is old and what is new in the influx of priests to America, lest their uninformed views about the past make matters worse for everyone.

On another topic, we ran into a central ecclesiological issue time after time: How uniform should Catholic worship be throughout the world, and how much should the church in each country be encouraged to adapt its expressions to fit the local culture? Before the Second Vatican Council, Catholic liturgy was something like the McDonald's of organized religion—the same everywhere. Later, people argued for letting the Mass take shape differently in each of the world's cultures.

How much uniformity and how much local inculturation is best? It is an unending issue. Most of our advisors recommended more local inculturation, not less, even though the recent signals from the Vatican have been in the opposite direction. They said that *at the very least* seminarians today need to learn to recognize and analyze cultural differences so that they will be able to move from culture to culture, making Catholic life spiritually nourishing in whatever setting they find themselves. Cultural specifics should be seen as integral, not extraneous, to liturgy and devotional life.

The overall topic of international priests boils down to two questions. Should Americans continue to bring in international priests? And, if so, what should be done to serve them and the American laity best? On the first question we heard fervid arguments pro and con, but be that as it may, we conclude that Americans in the future will bring in more international priests, not fewer, since the pressures are strong. Catholic leadership needs to prepare. Orientation programs must be expanded.

Recommendations, Long-Range and Short-Range

We asked everyone for recommendations. In our survey of international priests, the dominant recommendation given to us was that the church should provide them acculturation training, including instruction in English. This feeling was nearly unanimous.

The recommendations we solicited in interviews and focus groups were quite diverse. We will present eight of them which we heard repeatedly and which warrant attention. Two of them should be seen as long-range goals, not anything achievable soon.

1. The priest shortage in the United States (defined in terms of lay expectations about priests) cannot be solved through bringing in international priests. The numbers are too low and the difficulties too great. International priests provide only a partial alleviation. The basic solution to the problem, in the view of some, requires widening the eligibility for priestly ordination to include women and married men. Another idea is to broaden the sacramental functions of deacons. Optional celibacy for diocesan priests is favored by the majority of American laity and priests, as shown in recent surveys. This issue of broadening eligibility, of course, lies beyond the borders of the United States and thus needs to be considered at the international level. As a result, we need to see the idea as something waiting for the longer term.

2. We saw that the international flow of priests is an instance of the brain drain in other professions and that an injustice results when a wealthy nation brings in a priest who was trained by a developing nation at that nation's expense. Bishops and provincials in developing nations are unable to train and support all the priests their seminaries could produce. We conclude that some kind of international rule could be established in worldwide Catholicism, such that the wealthy Catholic nations provide funds to the poor nations to help them train and maintain ministerial leadership. If a priest is brought to Europe or the United States and incardinated, the receiving bishop should be obligated to pay the church in the developing nation for that man's education. In addition, the Catholics in the wealthy nations need to support their sister churches in the poor nations in every way possible.

The other six recommendations are different. They are feasible in the immediate future and should be seen as agendas for this year and next. All six received so much support that we can speak of a near consensus.

1. Follow the rules, as much as possible, in the American bishops' *Guidelines for Receiving Pastoral Ministers in the United States,* published in 1999. We heard it commended on all sides and believe that it should be heeded.

2. Begin orienting the priests in their home country before they arrive on our shores. Instruct them about the church in America and the diocese in which they will be working. Give them realistic appraisals of the opportunities and also the problems they will face; returned missionary priests who served in America may be available to do the training. At the same time, assess the candidates' English skills and postpone the coming of any men with weak English or extreme accents that Americans would not understand. Possibly a standardized test of English would be useful.

3. Prepare the receiving American pastor and parish for the coming of an international priest. Publicize the incoming priest's background, education, and talents, and meet with the laity to introduce him ahead of time. Send experts to consult with the pastor about common problems that international priests face. After the priest's arrival, sponsor welcoming meetings or mixers with parishioners and staff.

4. Expand and improve the orientation programs for incoming international priests. The programs should be local or regional, and a session should be held soon after the man arrives, then one, two, or three sessions in the ensuing year. Make participation in an orientation program mandatory.

5. Assign a mentor or companion to each incoming international priest to help him understand the dozens of practical and cultural problems he faces. Announce the name of the mentor publicly.

6. Consult with the international priests about their needs. Bishops' committees and diocesan committees should have ongoing liaison with them. One priest recommended having a national forum each year or two for international priests to hear about their experiences and recommendations.

We recognize that the American bishops today are faced with financial limitations. Diocesan staffs are being cut in many parts of the nation today, and new initiatives may not be possible just now. But the situation is urgent, and whatever can be done *should be done* for the good of the international priests and also the American church. The future is open.

Commentary

Rev. Anthony McGuire

In 1997 Richard P. McBrien wrote a column in the *National Catholic Reporter* entitled "Importing Priests to the US: a Poor Solution." It is excerpted in this book. When I read the article in 1997, I agreed with it. My reaction had a lot to do with my pride and lack of historical perspective. Also, I failed to recognize the changing scene of immigration into the United States as well as the diminishing number of priests in relation to a rapidly expanding number of laypeople in the church in the United States.

As a priest of the Archdiocese of San Francisco, I was proud of the fact that by the time I was ordained in 1965, the vast majority of the priests were native to the Archdiocese. In the first chapter of this book, William Smith cites the statistic that in 1963, one-third of the pastors in the Archdiocese of San Francisco were born and educated in Ireland. This may be true, but most of them were in the last years of their ministry and would soon be replaced by American-born pastors.

My experience of the Irish priests who came to San Francisco was positive. Over the years they had accompanied the immigrants with great dedication, they had provided tremendous leadership in the labor movement, they had built many new parishes to keep up with the exploding California population, and many had left a strong priestly role model for those who came after them. But I was proud that the new generation was native-born. I was proud that the Catholic Foreign Mission Society of America, Maryknoll, was sending fifty and sixty men and women a year to South America, Asia, and Africa. In those days, "Maryknoll" was a household word among American Catholics. Though that American pride and sense of self-sufficiency were well placed in one way, it also served as an obstacle to see the reality of the needs of the church in the United States.

In 1965, the same year I was ordained, Congress passed legislation favoring immigration from parts of the world other than Western Europe. Within a few decades, the huge influx from Mexico, Central and South America, Asia, and Africa changed the entire landscape of the U.S. church population. It became clear that the church in the United States needed immigrant priests to accompany the immigrant people. The Archdiocese of San Francisco felt the impact particularly of the immigration of Hispanics, Filipinos, Chinese, Koreans, and Vietnamese. This influx was taking place throughout the entire country, and bishops were scrambling to respond pastorally to it.

More challenging still was the fact that this influx, as well as an increase of Catholic population generally, was happening at the time when priests were leaving the ministry and the numbers entering the seminary were down. It was not until 1998, when I arrived at the National Conference of Catholic Bishops (NCCB) to work as director of Pastoral Care for Migrants and Refugees, that I became aware of the great need for priests and the complexity of the situation. Not only were priests being invited to accompany immigrants but also to become integrated into local churches as part of the presbyterate to serve the entire diocese. What the Second Vatican Council had declared had become a reality, namely, that every local church is not only a sending church but a receiving church. To be a missionary church is not only to send but also to receive. This is the reality that the church in the United States is facing.

As this book indicates, this is not a new reality. In its entire history, the Catholic Church in the United States has been a receiving church, dependent on clergy from abroad, first from Europe and now from all parts of the world. My experience of the predominance of native clergy in the San Francisco Archdiocese in the 1960s was but a small bleep on a very large screen. A very significant contribution of the present book is that it gives a broad historical context to the reality of international priests.

But to receive clergy from throughout the world is not without complications, nor can a receiving church invite priests from different cultures, with different languages and different customs, into its midst without a good deal of planning and preparation. This is another great contribution of the present work. It analyzes the extent of the reality of international priests in the United States, methodically reviews the positives and negatives of their presence, and explores creative ways to enhance their ministry.

This study also challenges leaders of dioceses and parishes to develop a pro-active consciousness about international priests, and it recommends important ways to facilitate their incorporation into the local church. If international priests are coming to the United States, they need to feel welcome, and they need to be oriented to the new circumstances. The priests with whom they serve need to know more about them and their culture. The American priests must welcome them as brothers and help them to be integrated into the local clergy. The people in the parishes in which they serve also need to be educated to the importance of this new minister, and they must come to understand the culture from which he comes. The arrival to a parish of a priest from a different land affords everybody the opportunity to come to know the reality of church ministry in the United States and in another part of the world.

Shortly after I undertook my ministry as director of Pastoral Care for Migrants and Refugees for the National Conference of Catholic Bishops, I began to develop a much more positive attitude toward international priests. I often attended national meetings of African, Asian, Hispanic, and Pacific Islands priests. The priests who attended those meetings impressed me as dedicated, hardworking men who were willing to suffer a great deal for the spreading of the gospel.

I recognized some of the difficulties I had experienced when I went to Hong Kong for several years as a Maryknoll Associate Priest. My first experience of Hong Kong was pure excitement. It was a beautiful city with a great level of culture and vitality. Day and night people were out in the street, shopping or selling, eating in sidewalk cafes, and running to the underground for their work. It was always a delight to be out walking around the city. But after three months of learning Cantonese and not doing well at it, of being away from my family and close friends, of faulty communications with local Chinese, after the humidity kicked in from April to October, a low-grade depression began to sink in, and I found myself oftentimes angry and unhappy. My daily prayer was for help to continue in the mission and not to waver. And help came, often through the Maryknoll priests, religious co-workers, and people in the parish in which I was living. After a while I adjusted to my limitations and the limitations of the situation, and I developed a more even disposition. That experience helped me appreciate the sacrifice and service of the international priests. This book indicates that some of the international priests come for money. Some send their money back home to support their families, but generally, in my judgment, they are no more driven to accumulate money than the local clergy are.

The other part of the Maryknoll experience was that in preparation for my time in Hong Kong, I spent three months at Maryknoll, New York, with four other priests who were in the same program and thirty laypeople who were going on mission as lay volunteers. The one thing I clearly remember about that preparation was that I was told of the stages I would experience as a missionary: excitement in the new place, followed by depression, followed by a realistic attitude toward one's capabilities in a new place. I was reminded to build into my life prayer, healthy friendships, and outside interests as well as the missionary activity. There were courses about the theology of mission, about culture, about service in areas of violence, about the posture of a missionary to new cultures, and about the baggage an American brings to a new land.

Of all the recommendations that the present study offers, the one I would underline is the importance of preparation for new ministers coming to the United States. Of all the possibilities, the one I prefer is to invite men to take their philosophical and theological training in the seminary that corresponds to the diocese they will be serving. The seminary experience serves as an acculturation process for them. Not only do they learn theology in their new language, but in their pastoral training they come to experience the role laypeople play in the local church, the way women participate in pastoral teams, and hopefully a spirit of collegiality that exists among priests, deacons, religious, and laypeople. The priests begin to have a sense of how organizations and committees work in a parish and how laypeople, often well-educated and experienced, engage in parish life. They come to know members of the local clergy with whom they will collaborate in the future and, it is hoped, will receive a fraternal welcome among them.

More often than not, the international priest arrives on the scene already ordained, a stranger in a strange land. This study makes clear that it is not an adequate pastoral response to think that a priest is the same anywhere in the world, that he can be brought from a rural African parish to an inner-city or suburban parish in the United States without any preparation. One issue that needs to become part of universal personnel practice is the requirement of good orientation for the international priest, for his pastor, and for the people he will be serving. This study describes several of these programs throughout the country, some more comprehensive and successful than others. The reality is that these programs, still in their initial stages, are very uneven in their demands. They are not promoted by all bishops, and not all are compulsory for international priests. It is not likely that each diocese can have such a program, but a region or a state could provide an orientation program. The greatest service this study can do for the church in the United States is to encourage and expand these orientation programs in all regions of the country.

As these programs increase, a useful universal curriculum will emerge. Some issues will be tackled by the local parish, including the practical issues of surviving in a new context: finances, transportation, buying a car, language study, food, and shelter. The new international priest will challenge the local clergy to figure out ways of making him feel at home, ways that correspond to the culture of the new priest—rice over potatoes, soccer over football. And the new priest will need to make efforts to be at home for meals, to gather before dinner together or at the end of the day. Other issues will fall to the local diocese: health and auto insurance, spiritual direction, diocesan policies.

Still other topics are broader. The introduction to the theology, the pastoral practices that drive the local parishes, the comparison of the new culture with the culture from which the priest has come, and the way the United States has incorporated the changes of the Second Vatican Council—all these need a more comprehensive, integrated approach that demands more time and a process of learning that allows for sharing experiences. The most successful programs use models of adult learning which avoid a lecture style and which combine input from a mentor with personal reflection and group discussion.

Two areas of adjustment are very difficult. One pertains to roles. The role the priest plays in his own culture is often very different from the role he plays in the United States. Many of the Asian cultures in particular are much more conscious of the importance of an authority figure and give that person much more status than he would be given in the United States. The elderly, the parent, the teacher, and the priest are all viewed with reverence. Respect is automatically given to a person because of his role. In the Catholic context, this gives a special comfort level to the priest; it provides easy access to families, emotional support, and sometimes financial support through free services, gifts, and invitations to dinners and social events. In the United States, by contrast, a person is generally accepted and respected, not because of his role, but because of his performance. It can be difficult for international priests to break out of their cultural comfort zone and face the new, more challenging context. Many have done so and have won American friends who recognize the effort required to serve in a new situation, but many other international priests find it daunting.

Another sometimes intractable problem is spoken accent, an issue that this study confronts head-on. Sometimes the recommended program dealing with accent works, but sometimes it doesn't. In the revised liturgy an equal emphasis is placed on the Liturgy of the Word and the Liturgy of the Eucharist, and central to the Liturgy of the Word is the homily. Many people come to church looking for a word from the Lord to help them get through their week, to renew their drooping spirits. If they see the priest with the heavy accent coming into the sanctuary at the beginning of Mass, their spirits droop. Frustrated as well is the priest himself. He realizes right away that he is turning off the people with his accent. In one parish I insisted that on Sunday a deacon preach when the priest with the heavy accent said the Mass, though I knew this was taken as a putdown to the priest.

In summary, this book makes a significant contribution to working through a very complex pastoral problem in the church in the United States. It reviews the many issues, trying to separate truth from rumor or prejudice. One of the strengths of the study is the use of direct quotes from the people interviewed. This gives it a very real feel. It is clearly based on the day-to-day lives of the people involved on all sides of this issue. Another strength of the study is the series of recommendations which, if put to use, would make a real difference in the integration of international priests into the church in the United States. Those who prepared the study have worked very hard over a long period and should be proud of the contribution they have made.

Rev. Anthony E. McGuire has served the Archdiocese of San Francisco as vicar for the Spanish-speaking and secretary for Ethnic and Cultural Affairs. He has worked for the National Conference of Catholic Bishops as director of Pastoral Care for Migrants and Refugees. At present he is pastor of St. Matthew's, a multicultural parish in San Mateo, California.

Commentary

Dr. Seung Ai Yang

Catholics in the United States have been witnessing new faces both in the pew and at the altar, but more often than bringing joy and excitement, it has brought frustration and struggle. This study of international priests, with its rich data and well-crafted research and replete with valuable insights, provides a great resource to the church. The authors focus on two questions: whether more international priests be brought into the United States, and if so, how.

The seemingly simple yes-or-no format of the first question is misleading, for the topic is actually more complicated and difficult. As this study repeatedly reveals, the first question is intimately related to more fundamental concerns in ecclesiology, such as vocation, holy orders, the role of deacons, women's ordination, and lay leadership. The question is not self-standing and requires broader research and deeper collective deliberation. In fact, more international priests will be brought in anyway, as this study concludes (p. 94). The current increase of immigration also confirms this conclusion. Therefore, in my response I will focus on the second question: *how*. But let me first offer a brief comment on the question of *whether*.

I would like to emphasize that, as voiced by several people in this study, the shortage of priests should not be considered the principal reason for bringing in international priests. First, regardless of the problem of the shortage of priests, international priests will continue coming to the United States. The new wave of immigration to the United States after the 1960s, the increase of Catholics in the United States, and globalization will all contribute to the increasing number of international priests. Second, as the data in this study suggest, the United States has a much lower ratio of laity to priests than the countries from which the international priests come (Figure 3.1, p. 30). Indeed, those countries are generally where missionaries are most needed (see the authors' discussion of Philip Jenkins' *The*

Next Christendom on pp. 28–32). Third, inviting international priests as the solution to the shortage leads some U.S. Catholics to blame the presence of international priests for hindering the promotion of their current ecclesiological concerns, such as the marriage option for priests, lay ministry, women's ordination, and so on. Fourth, if the shortage of priests is presented as the principal reason for bringing in international priests, the priests are easily but unjustly considered mere "second-class fill-ins" (p. 66), because American Catholics in general prefer American-born priests.

In responding to the question of *how,* I will begin with a reflection on a fundamental question about priestly vocation. Then, after discussing the different contexts of international priests and American Catholics, I will comment on the concept of acculturation as a mutual process. Finally, I will offer some practical suggestions.

I. Priesthood as Vocation versus Occupation

One of the things that struck me while reading this study is the frequent strong market-language used by the study participants in describing the church in general and the priesthood in particular. While I acknowledge that the church as an institution must deal with financial matters, expressions such as "competitive religious market" for the church and "import," "pay for them," "employment," "job" or other capitalist terms, tones, and ideas for the priesthood deeply concerned me. I had to ponder whether these capitalist words might indicate a general understanding of priesthood simply as an occupation rather than a vocation, even among priests. In my eleven years of seminary teaching in the United States, I have always emphasized the importance of priesthood as a vocation, as a divine call to the divine mission, requiring a fully committed life to the mission in response, just as we find in the calling and response of the prophets in the Old Testament and the apostles in the New Testament. Believing that this is still what the church expects me to teach, I would like to share my reflections:

- This study clearly points out that it is poor countries that most need missionaries today and in the near future. The current trend that priests prefer to come to affluent countries for ministry is to be seriously examined from the perspective of priestly vocation and the mission of the church.

- This study reveals in several places that people often use the economic status of parishioners as the standard to differentiate good and bad parishes. A parish is even described as "garbage," apparently because it is a poor parish (p. 91). I am afraid that this shocking phenomenon is not an isolated example; rather, it reflects the capitalist ethos of our society in general, which has also affected our church. Again, I would like to recommend that it be critically examined in relation to priestly vocation and the mission of the church.

- If priesthood is a divine call to the divine mission requiring a full-life commitment substantiated by God's special gift of celibacy, it should not be understood as an occupation to choose as a means to support one's own family financially.

- Financial agreements should be made on the diocesan level between the sending and receiving bishops. The case of the Diocese of Richmond and the diocese in the Philippines is an excellent example (p. 80).

II. Different Contexts of American Catholics and International Priests

Human beings are cultural products. Culture shapes what we think and how we behave. It construes patterns of thought and mindset for people who have shared their history and traditions. Although each individual within the same cultural group thinks and behaves differently because of different social locations such as education, gender, age, experience, family, religion, and class, some cultural patterns are still discernible in each group. Understanding each other's cultural contexts, therefore, is greatly helpful when an international priest and an American parish want to build a community together. By understanding each other's contexts, both sides can understand why they think and behave the way they do. At the risk of simplistic summary due to space limitations, I will examine two interrelated elements that I believe are important in understanding the different contexts of international priests and American Catholics: postcolonialism; migration, race, and ethnicity.

A. Postcolonialism

Today the majority of international priests come from developing countries in Asia, Africa, and Latin America. Most of these countries recently suffered from the colonization of Western powers and at the same time were introduced to various denominations of Christianity by the colonists. Even though most of these countries gained independence in the last century, they still suffer from exploitation and domination by Western powers. Cultural theorists use the term "postcolonialism" to describe ideas critiquing this phenomenon. "Postcolonial" has become the common context for today's world, so to speak. How does this postcolonial context affect international priests and American Catholics respectively?

International priests maintain the version of Christianity that was introduced by their colonists, since the people in power claimed it to be "universal truth" and dismissed native traditions and cultures as pagan. At the same time, the hierarchical and authoritative understanding of the church was even more consolidated in the soils of colonial subjects, who were raised with a strong tradition of hierarchy and patriarchy. This is the version of ecclesiology and theology that many international priests bring when they come to the United States. Since they understand this pre-Vatican version as "universal," they have difficulty in accepting the different understanding of the church among American Catholics. In short, as postcolonial subjects, they are often politically liberal (i.e., promoting equality) and theologically conservative (i.e., hierarchical, autocratic, and pre-Vatican).

American Catholics, as heirs of American history of the colonial era, revolution, independence, civil war, and social justice movements, value freedom, equality, and justice, on the one hand, and maintain the pride and mindset of victors, on the other. After the end of the cold war and the demise of the Soviet Union, the United States has virtually become the sole supreme power in the world, to the degree that "American imperialism" has become a serious concern for many intellectuals and activists in the world. In today's postcolonial context, the pride of Americans for their country as the supreme power is so strong that Americans often forget their history (see chapter 1 as a great example). They even have a tendency to consider anything "un-American" as inferior. The expressions "second-rate priest" or "second-class fill-ins" for international priests well reflect this mindset.

B. Migration, Race, and Ethnicity

Throughout human history people have migrated for various reasons: wars, food and water, safety, or a better life. In fact, the young nation of America was born out of a major migration in the modern era. All Americans are immigrants or descendants of immigrants except for Native Americans. Unfortunately, the U.S. immigration history, of which the history of international priests is a microcosm, parallels the U.S. history of white racism. Ever since the new nation was born, newer immigrants experienced discrimination through public policy and laws, as well as on a personal level. Once they were accepted as "Americans," however, newer immigrants joined the discriminatory game of group boundary-defense against newcomers. Western Europeans, Southern and Eastern Europeans, and Jews gradually became the "in-group" members of "Americans" and "white." However, people of darker skins, such as Native Americans, Asian immigrants, or blacks, were not accepted as "Americans," no matter how long they had lived in the country.

It was not until the mid-twentieth century that those of darker skins were granted the same rights as Americans and "whites," at least legally (e.g., land-owning, voting, immigration, and desegregation). In other words, the discriminatory game of group boundary of "American" versus "un-American" has been intimately related to skin color and the mythical concept of race and ethnicity.

The undeniable, tragic reality is that white racism is still an everyday experience for people living in America, even if it is *de jure* a thing of the past. As a matter of fact, today's subtle discrimination is more painful than blunt expressions for many people of darker skins. As an example, a friend of mine, a fourth-generation Chinese immigrant, frequently gets the following questions from "Americans," revealing the assumption that she must not be an American: "You speak English so well. Where did you learn your English?" or "Where are you from?" The U.S. Catholic Church is not an exception, and because it is a faith community that supposedly practices the belief that all are equal and one in Christ (cf. Gal 3:26-29), the pain and wound of those who experience discrimination could be even deeper. International priests of darker skins, even after naturalization or incardination, or even American-born Asian priests are usually viewed by "American" Catholics as un-American, un-white, strange, "international," and foreign. They are considered as belonging to an inferior race and ethnicity and not acceptable to the "in" group of "American" Catholics.

White racism is a shamefully integral part of today's American culture, and American Catholics often unconsciously judge an international priest on the basis of his race and ethnicity. Throughout the pages of this study, one witnesses the voices of "Americans" who stereotype international priests by their race and ethnicity and those of international priests who painfully share their experiences of racial discrimination.

III. Acculturation as Mutual Process

In addressing the question of *how* priests of other countries should be brought in, this study reports the words of many who emphasize the importance of the acculturation and orientation of international priests. As much as I agree on its importance, I believe that we must deliberate on the meaning of "acculturation" first if we don't want to perpetuate the postcolonial tragedy.

What do we mean by acculturation of international priests? If we mean that we teach them to think and behave just like "American" Catholics, it is not only unfeasible but also unethical. It is unfeasible because, as discussed above, one's patterns of thought and behavior are cumulatively shaped by one's cultural location through a long shared history and traditions. The cultural locations of international priests and American Catholics are quite different. It is unethical because it often requires international priests to deny who they are and to abandon the "home" traditions that have nourished them. This is actually a hidden expression of cultural imperialism patronizing the international priests.

If acculturation means a process that helps international priests to be capable of ministering to Catholics in America and to advance the mission of the church while keeping their integrity as who they are, then it must happen in both directions. For the sake of convenience, let us imagine an American parish of predominantly white members that receives an international priest. Both the international priest and the parish community need to learn the differences of their cultural contexts to understand why they think and behave in the ways they do. Understanding the different contexts will involve self-reflection. The international priest might find that he is internalizing the colonists' version of Christianity as well as the mindset of colonists insisting that it is "universal." The parish community could find that they are, in spite of themselves, racists who judge people based on skin color and have a tendency to look down upon different cultures and ideas, believing that their own is superior or absolutely correct. Both sides might realize that when one blames the other for narrow-mindedness and rigidity, it is actually oneself who is narrow-minded or rigid.

The self-reflections, then, enable us to understand why we think and behave differently and to make room for listening and acknowledging different voices and cultures. We then find the need to be willing to negotiate to find our common ground. The negotiation should be made on the basis of the gospel and the mission of the church, which will lead the people not to impose their own culturally bound ideas as absolutely correct or "universal." We will also be able to understand that the differences among us are often God's gracious gift to us to recognize the limitedness of our nature and to recover from it by learning from each other and working together. Then we will no longer hate or blame others for our differences but will be able to give thanks to our God, who graciously provided us with abundant diversity.

IV. Some Practical Suggestions

- If the shortage of priests is the only reason for inviting an international priest, he should not be invited. It will merely perpetuate the problems reported in this study. Also, if a priest is invited, it will be important to inform the parishioners that he is coming because of his qualifications, not just as a fill-in.

- For helping the international priest with information and the skills necessary for American life, such as driving, getting a car, reporting income tax, opening a bank account, etc., a formal orientation does not seem to be the best setting, as it can be overwhelming to a newcomer. Instead, ongoing support from a group of people easily accessible to the new priest would be more beneficial, since life in a new setting will constantly bring new questions. One possibility is that a parish could form a hospitality team of several volunteers, with a chairperson responsible for organizing the volunteers' schedule and functioning as a contact person. The priest should be urged to contact the team chair when he has any specific questions about his new life in America. The team may be dismissed once the priest has settled relatively well.

- When planning a support program for international priests, it would be valuable to include international priests as speakers to share the wisdom gained from their actual experiences. For example, they could share some critical (or life-threatening) incidents and some thanksgiving (or life-giving) incidents. Or they could share some "dos" and "don'ts" based on their concrete experiences. It would also be helpful to diversify the international priest-speakers, especially according to the length of their U.S. ministry. For example, a priest who has just finished his first year of ministry might provide vivid examples for the new priests to expect. A priest who has ministered five years may share a different perspective, including the changes from the first year to more settled ministry life. A priest who feels quite at home after many years of ministry might give not only wisdom but also a realistic hope to the newcomers who have difficulty imagining the feeling of being "at home" in a new land.

- Before or after the arrival of the international priest, it would be very beneficial to have a reflection session for his parishioners about their own historical and social location as Catholics in America, including a very brief history of immigration, international priests, and racism in the United States. The reflection session might also include a practical guide of "dos" and "don'ts" in relation to the international priest. For example: "Do" encourage the priest to share his traditions, value systems, food, etc. "Don't" impose something on the priest, saying that he should do it because he is in America.

- The priest also needs a reflection session on his historical and social location as a Catholic priest who comes to the United States for ministry.

Dr. Seung Ai Yang is associate professor of Sacred Scripture at the St. Paul Seminary School of Divinity, University of St. Thomas, St. Paul, Minnesota.

Commentary

Rev. Michael Heher

I.

More than twenty years ago, as I was preparing to go abroad for the first time, a wise Mexican Jesuit wrote me a long and beautiful letter in Spanish, in which, with great delicacy, he tried to warn me about what was going to happen. He was not concerned about how I would deal with the rigors of theological academia, as I had expected from an alumnus of the university where I was going to study. Rather, he tried to tell a good-hearted but very inexperienced American how disoriented I would feel, adjusting for the first time to living in a land with a language and a culture not my own. He was right, of course, and, as he had predicted in his letter, it was the best thing that could have happened to me at that time. It was an undeserved grace.

I did not understand this when I first read his letter. Until I moved out of my own culture, I had no idea that I was actually embarrassingly myopic. My own culture was precisely what I took for granted. It was the "is" in "the way it is," or so it seemed to someone who only saw it from the inside.

We Americans, as a group, are particularly well known for cultural insularity. Perhaps it has something to do with being a people who live from sea to shining sea; we are so vast and diverse that we don't notice the really foreign among us or, when we do, don't care for it unless and until it is swirled into the "melting pot," at which point its foreign flavor is sufficiently softened. Yes, we are a people who consume alien cuisine to an extent unknown almost anywhere else: Chinese take-out one day, burritos in the microwave the next? Even our fundraising is ecumenical, with handmade tamales on sale after Mass and spaghetti dinners served in the parish hall. We are the ones whose congregations respond generously over and over again to missionaries with heart-breaking tales from the developing world. And now we rival the Japanese in our international touring.

In my present circumstances, I frequently find myself at various affairs at a table of strangers, and I never fail to spark a conversation by asking them where they have been or where they hope to visit. And yet, for all this, too many of us still like the world too much on our own terms, secretly preferring the comfort and convenience of the Paris Hotel and Casino in Las Vegas for the authentic City of Light with its strange language, supposedly rude waiters, and impenetrable customs. We take the jalapeños off the nachos when our Mexican neighbors aren't looking. We like the exotic kiss, but we aren't ready for a committed embrace. We do not expect such experiences to change us in any essential ways; rather, we reassure ourselves that globalization will make the rest of the world more and more like us.

That may be why the first thing we notice about the "international priest" is his noticeable accent, his feeble English fluency. We expect him to become one of us and to be quick about it. I know, as I am now one of those who get the phone calls and e-mails at the chancery: "Doesn't the bishop think our parish is important enough to be assigned a real priest?" I also hear our priests talking about international priests occasionally simply in terms of the amount of work they can get out of them: "You know that Father Gilberto you sent me? He's not exactly a pastoral powerhouse." Now, in this enlightening study, we learn that the international priests themselves know that this is the way many of us think about them. It calls for a change of heart on our part.

Why was welcoming them with open arms not the first thing on our minds? Why did we fail to notice how generous they have been when, for whatever set of mixed motives, they left behind family and country to serve here? What blindness prevented us from noticing the fear in their eyes, their genuine amazement at our way of life, and most of all their loneliness? And when they dared—which most often they did not—to point out our materialism, our preoccupations with time and wealth and the individual will, why were we defensive rather than ashamed? Despite everything that Pope John Paul II tried to tell us, a vast crowd of us still will not acknowledge the many ways our own society is un-Christian. It is like what the rich man is told in the Gospel: If they did not listen to Moses and Elijah, they will not listen even if someone comes to them from Ghana or Vietnam or Guatemala.

While there is much that is worrisome in the American culture, there is also a great deal about the church here that is impressive. For a number of years young Irish priests in teaching assignments would come out in the summers to get a California tan (which ended up on them having a decidedly red tint) and to renew their faith in the Vatican II church. They came here because they wanted to be part of a church in which liturgies were well celebrated, where they could see, even in the summer, hundreds of people involved in everything from fundraising to hospice care.

One reason for this vitality may be that the Catholic Church has been in a minority position in society for most of its history in the United States.

That blunted and still blunts clericalism among the clergy and self-satis-faction among the laity. Catholics here both inherit and choose their faith. In a secular and polyvalent dominant culture, few will look down on you if instead of going to pray at church, you sleep in on Sunday morning or work out at the gym, especially in urban and suburban areas. But neither is the public at large impressed if you go. You go because it works for you or you want to see how to make it work for you. This process of growing ownership has produced a flowering of lay involvement in ministry, both professional and volunteer, and a needed expansion of the role of laity and religious in ecclesiastical leadership. In many parishes you hear it in the singing and see it in the many items pressing for space in the bulletin.

A couple of years ago a friend of mine was summoned, while vacationing in Rome, to an audience with a Vatican official. I forget the pretext for the appointment, as it was hardly discussed; the main purpose of the interview became clear enough as the official detailed the many wrongs, errors, and forms of blindness of the Catholic clergy, religious, and people in the United States. After listening politely to his complaints for a long while, my friend finally became impatient and said: "What you say may be true. I'm not in a position to say. But I do know this: our churches are full and yours are not."

II.

International priests here serve in very distinct kinds of circumstances, and any sophisticated effort to help them adjust will need to attend to this. One priest becomes an itinerant trying to find Portuguese-speaking shep-herds who wander, true nomads, across vast rangelands with their herds. A priest from Myanmar finds himself the pastor of two small rural parishes in Kansas, hundreds of miles away from contact with others of his native country. But a Mexican priest, serving in East Los Angeles, would be able to live in his language and culture comfortably for years: fresh tortillas are a block away; the supermarket carries the hot sauces he loves. Pity, if you wish, the older Vietnamese priest who, used to the simplicity of a country parish, finds himself living in a huge convention center of a parish, like my own, that zips along in three languages at a dizzying pace, with numerous, overlapping forms of lay collaboration and leadership.

As a longstanding member of our priests' personnel board, I want to un-derscore one of this study's conclusions, namely, that international priests should stay for an extended period of time. There remain in our urban areas a certain number of neighborhood parishes that are almost exclusively made up of a single ethnic community or shared language. But this is and will be less and less the case. Where I live, Koreans live in apartments and buy condos and homes next to Anglos, who find themselves next to Viet-namese, Salvadoran, and Mexican immigrants. Yes, in some parishes the work is still divided among the priests and staff strictly according to language or culture—an appropriate strategy in the first generation of migration—but as their local ties grow and their children learn English in school, the members of these communities drift. They become strong and confident of themselves enough to mix it up with those outside their language and culture, to welcome a life that includes neighbors, co-workers, and parishioners outside their ethnic community. Some of their elders decry such moves and try to get their priests to agree with them, but it rarely works; people's attractions are spontaneous. And so priests willing to work only in their native tongue among their own people will be less useful to them.

Recently at a May crowning before one of our Vietnamese-language Masses, I noticed some tall Anglos gawking at the spectacle with me and wondered why they were there. Then, as the dancing began, I saw in the back a young girl dressed with a flower crown and long white dress, just like the others, but her hair was blond and her eyes blue. She was even singing along with the Vietnamese hymn to Mary, though she could not possibly have known what it meant. Was she brought in because they were short one girl, or had a Vietnamese friend's enthusiasm caught her fancy? It doesn't matter. She was there and nobody said a word about it. Rather, an elderly Polish parishioner asked me why this event was not listed in the bulletin and said, "I think a lot of us would love to have known about it."

A real shepherd of the people knows not just how they were but how they are now. He is prepared to share with them the intuitive act of a people keeping what they love alive by allowing it to change in authentic, enlivening, and welcoming ways. He helps them to sing the songs of home and to compose songs that make this new place home. This is not the task of a short-timer. By the time he gets settled, he'll already be packing his bags for his return to his native land.

III.

I should have known better, but I was one of those pastors who lamely imagined that "a priest is a priest is a priest" when the first international priest was assigned to my parish. It was a sign of my respect for him that I trusted he knew what to do, or so I believed. When he was slow to answer sick calls, I did not explain to him that in America, for better or for worse, people expect requests such as these to be honored pronto. Speed is one of our cultural biases. It didn't even occur to me to mention it. I simply presumed that the priest knew what he was supposed to do and chose not to do it, that he could not be bothered to serve the people properly. As you can imagine, it did not work out well.

And so I was careful not to make the same mistake when the next international priest was assigned to my parish. Although he was trained at a local seminary and spoke barely accented English, he was unsure whether the many staff members were threats or perks. When I asked him about statements he had made to a female staff member that had offended her, he answered, "So? I'm the priest. You should be defending me. Who is she?" I said she was a professional with as many academic degrees as he had and many more years of dedicated pastoral experience, that's who she was. Thus began an awkward but necessary conversation about our perceptions of the place and value of women in both our cultures.

One of the great strengths of my own culture is that we can talk about anything. Yes, this leads to the excesses of tabloid headlines, talk shows where people throw chairs at each other, and vivid commercials for pharmaceuticals to aid those with erectile dysfunction. But darkness is brought to light, with an openness that other cultures cannot fathom, by frank discussions about the abuse of drugs and alcohol, about the threats to children and elders, about private concerns that benefit from a public airing. Americans love the one who tells it like it is, warts and all. In the safe haven of therapy or in conversations among intimates, in the honest communication between spouses and friends, souls are bared, bonds are strengthened, and understanding replaces blindness. It is one of the ways we have discovered to keep our culture alive.

We have in our hands now this study, which suggests the broad outlines of a discussion that needs to take place between the native clergy and our international missionaries. I welcome the light these conversations could bring, but will we really have them? I'm not so sure. If ever there was a system designed to avoid conversation about any number of important matters, it is the slam-bam roller-coaster of priestly ministry in most of our parishes. We don't even eat together anymore. And among priests from different cultures, even more excuses are at the ready for not talking and listening to each other.

In my own individualistic culture, one of the worst offenses is meddling, telling someone else what to do. So I keep quiet about my concerns, except on my days off among my friends. In the cultures of many international priests, one of the worst offenses is to contradict or question a superior. One must agree even when he really disagrees. And so I hear "Yes" when yes is not meant, or more often I get no answer at all. In a rectory filled with such respectful silences, hardly anyone laughs, let alone kids another. It's not the kind of place where you might share a drink or watch the news together or go out to a late dinner on Sunday night. It doesn't sound like much fun. The practice of Catholic priesthood is becoming lonelier enough nowadays for other reasons. If you ask me, I vote for more communication, despite the difficulties across cultures. And I ask God to give us more honesty and more courage.

Rev. Michael Heher is the vicar general and moderator of the curia of the Diocese of Orange, California. He has a doctorate in theology from the Pontifical Gregorian University in Rome. His essays have appeared in *America, Church,* and *Image.* A book of his essays, *The Lost Art of Walking on Water: Reimagining the Priesthood,* was published by Paulist Press (2004).

Commentary

Rev. Virgilio Elizondo

First of all, I would like to thank the authors of this study for the opportunity of reviewing their excellent work. It is a very honest and objective presentation of the status of priests from other countries ministering within the United States. As the authors mentioned, in many ways there is nothing new about this. Priests from other countries have always come to serve in our country. In many ways we have been considered a mission territory in need of missioners. So really there is nothing new.

The amazing fact is that we are still in need of priest missioners. We ourselves have been sending priests to other countries, yet today we are crying for help. What does this say about our own Catholic Church in the United States? As is evident from the responses, there is no agreement on this point. Yet the fact is clear that we will continue to look for priests from other countries, as we had in the past, to minister in our country.

What is totally new about the present-day situation is that whereas before, priests came from European countries that in many ways are the roots of our own U.S. cultural way of life and therefore could more easily adapt to the culture of the "frontier" emerging in America, today's priests coming to serve in the United States are from countries with totally different cultural ways of life, values, and religious expression.

You might well say that in former times—since the beginning of the great European colonial expansion in the sixteenth century—priests went as missioners from the rich and developed countries to the poor and underdeveloped countries, from what was perceived as the center of civilization and Catholicism to the exotic frontiers. Nobody referred to them as "international priests"—they were simply Catholic missioners! Often their knowledge of the local language was so bad that they had to preach and instruct through a native interpreter. This is still taking place today. Yet the people did not complain. They might enjoy a few laughs because of the linguistic *faux pas* of the missioner, but they did not complain, nor did the missioner feel unqualified because his language was so horrible! After all, these men came from "the developed and civilized center of the world," or at least so they thought. So who cared if they could not speak correctly or could not understand the ways and customs of the native people, for after all they had come to evangelize and civilize. I know this mentality has changed drastically since Vatican II, but it still persists among some.

Today the very reverse is taking place. The priests are not coming from the rich, dominant, and imposing cultures of the world; they are coming from among the poorest of today's world. At this point I found a serious fault with the study. It did not distinguish, except in the case of Korean priests, between priests who come to serve the people of our country at large and priests who come from Mexico and Latin America to serve their own people who are now making their home in the United States. It is the teaching of our church that priests and religious should accompany migrants on their journeys to new lands. One category of priests is those who come to serve the native people of this land, and another category is those that come to serve their own people who have migrated to this country. It is a very different dynamic, and there will definitely be very different pastoral needs.

Priests Coming to Serve the Community at Large

In relation to priests coming to serve the people at large, that is, the mainline, English-speaking Catholic population, I would say that the major challenge is with the receiving community. We Americans are well known for our subconscious arrogance in assuming that our way in all things is the right way for everyone. There is no doubt about our generosity toward people in need, yet the collective consciousness that we are the best and most powerful country in the world gives us a certain discomfort with people who are different or speak differently. We see others as adjusting to us, but we do not see ourselves as adjusting to others. We find it very difficult to even tolerate difference in any form.

Hence, rather than being grateful for the generosity of the poor in sending us some of their priests, we complain because they are different or speak somewhat differently. If we are going to continue inviting priests from other countries, especially the poor countries of the world, to come and work among us, we need first of all to prepare the parish spiritually and culturally for the joy of receiving a priest from one of the poor countries of the world. We need to speak about the beauty of difference, how difference can enrich every one of us. Furthermore, we need to address this evangelically; after all, it is through the "little (insignificant) people" of the world that God continues to evangelize all, but especially the rich and the powerful of the world. (Luke 10:21-22; Matt 11:25-30; 1 Cor 1:18-30). Will we in the United States have the humility to accept this? A great pastoral challenge!

In response to the generosity of the churches of the poor countries that are willing to send priests to us, we should respond by sending local pastors along with some parishioners to work in the area from which those priests are coming. This was suggested by one of the respondents, and it was an excellent suggestion. Americans as a whole tend to be very provincial. We have no idea of either the misery of poverty or the beautiful values that are lived by other peoples around the world. We may have a lot to teach others in the area of technology and other material areas, but they have so much to teach us spiritually! So rather than just receiving priests from the poor countries of the world, we should work toward an exchange program.

Some would shout "Impossible!" Some would say that the very reason for inviting these priests is the priest shortage in the United States. If this is the only reason, it is very selfish. Ecclesial selfishness can be very dangerous. Do we really have a priest shortage, or have we been spoiled by too many priests? Latin America has had a very vibrant Catholicism for centuries, and the ratio of faithful per priest has been far larger than in America. Such an exchange of priests would be most enriching for the Catholicism of the United States. God would truly bless us if out of our own perceived scarcity we would be willing to do with less so that others in greater need could have more. Maybe the lack of ecclesial generosity is precisely what has been missing from our American church.

There is no doubt that any priest going to serve in another country should be prepared spiritually, culturally, and linguistically. Learning the language is not sufficient. One has to learn the ways and customs of the people so as to truly minister in the way of the Incarnation. What type of program will best do this can be discussed, but the fact that such programs of preparation are necessary is beyond question.

Priests Coming to Serve Their Own People

This study zeroed in on priests coming to serve the mainline English-speaking Catholics and did not take into serious account priests coming to accompany their immigrant brothers and sisters in our country. Since the study was conducted only in English, it failed to listen to the voices of the greatest number of priests coming from other countries, especially the Spanish-speaking ones.

One of the best ways that the Catholic Church helped immigrants from Europe gradually acculturate into the American way of life was by having their own priests and religious accompany them into our country. National parishes served their people for several generations before the people moved into mainline United States. Until World War II most of our parish communities were ethnic communities that ministered in the language and culture of the people. We did not have multilingual parishes, but rather a variety of different monolingual parishes in every diocese.

Today there is massive immigration from Mexico and Latin America. Most of the people coming are forced to immigrate because of the harsh economic conditions of their countries. They do not leave because they want to, but because they have no other option—either migrate or starve to death! They are economic refugees who are as oppressed as political refugees fleeing from Communist regimes. Yet in the United States they are often received as fleeing criminals! They do not feel welcome in most of our parishes. It is not that they are told, as in the old days, that they do not belong here, but the very body language of the parishioners tells them they are not wanted. Often it is the small Pentecostal and fundamental churches that are welcoming the immigrants in their own language and with their own music. In these small storefront churches they experience the welcome that is denied them in some of our Catholic churches.

Hence priests in Mexico and Latin American feel an obligation of accompanying their people. The Latin American bishops are becoming more and more aware of this pastoral obligation. It is not that the priests are abandoning their people in areas where priests are so scarce, but rather that they are accompanying their people in their flight from misery unto life. They are accompanying their people in their painful exodus into a land that needs them for cheap and unprotected labor but does not want to see them around. Americans would like to have the benefits of the low prices the immigrants make possible, but not the blessings of their personal presence in their churches and society.

So priests from Mexico and Latin America come, as priests from Ireland, Poland, Italy, Germany, and other places came in the past, to serve their own people in their new land in the United States. A seminary has been set up in Mexico City precisely to prepare priests to work in the United States. Programs at SEPI in Miami and MACC in San Antonio help incoming priests understand and appreciate the life, struggles, and hurdles the people face every day. Immigrants and their children have special pastoral needs that usually are not met or even suspected in the average parish. For priests coming from Mexico and Latin America to work with the Latin American people in the United States, English is useful but not an immediate priority. The most immediate priority is to minister to the people in ways that are respectful and meaningful to the people.

Yet these priests also need special preparation about the ways the church and society function in the United States. It is true that we are one Catholic Church, but the church functions in very different ways as it becomes incarnated in the various cultures of the world. One faith, but a multiplicity of expressions, customs, and priorities.

One thing that has become very clear over the years is that simply because a priest is from Spain or Latin America does not prepare him to work with the Spanish-speaking of the United States. In many cases, simply bringing in a Spanish-speaking priest disrupts a very active and dynamic lay apostolate. When people move to the United States, they begin to acculturate in many ways and are no longer the same as they were in Latin America. In many ways they remain very Latino/a, yet in many other ways they become very acculturated to the United States. For better or worse, they become something new, something different. Simply because a priest speaks Spanish does not prepare him to work well with Spanish-speaking Americans. More is needed.

What I think we need, something that I have been advocating for many years, is the formation of a "St. James Missionary Society" in reverse! Priests could join the society for a certain number of years, have a sufficient period of cultural, linguistic, and spiritual preparation, and then, in cooperation with the inviting diocese, determine the place and nature of their work. These priests could be visited regularly by the coordinator of the society, have regular regional meetings, and put on an annual retreat-meeting, where they could enjoy fellowship, pray together, discuss their work, and celebrate the Eucharist together. This would be the place where success stories could be shared, and difficulties and problems could be discussed openly. If need be, the superior of the society could then discuss the problem areas with the bishop of the diocese concerned.

I do not believe that the present way of doing things will work, that is, bishops recruiting directly from Colombia, Mexico, or other countries. It would be far better to have a well-planned program that could keep improving through the successes and failures of the participants.

The most urgent need for priests and religious is felt by the undocumented immigrants from Mexico and Latin America arriving daily. These are among the most vulnerable people in the world. The great majority of them are Catholic. They expose themselves to horrifying dangers, and many die in the process of attempting to cross into the United States. Once here, they have no one to go to, no one they can trust, and they are easily exploited by anyone. Society calls them illegals, yet we know that for Christ and his church there are no illegals. In fact, our attitude toward them will help determine our last judgment (Matt 25). These people have a far greater need for priests and religious than many of the parishioners in our urban and rural parishes. Yet it seems that the church does not want to be aware of the presence of the poorest of the poor among us. We do not seem to remember the words of Christ: "I was a stranger and you took me in."

Final Word

There are many other comments I could make, and I would love to enter into a serious conversation on this topic. But I will finish with a few brief comments. In my opinion, the term "international priests" is a misnomer. They should simply be recognized for what they are: missioners to the United States. Another point is deeper: Does this study mask the deepest issue: a healthy growth and development of our U.S. church would produce sufficient priests and religious to minister to our people and even to send some as missioners to other countries. We need to take a deep and honest look at ourselves and see what we have to do to develop the church in the United States.

This study, beyond the few limitations that I have pointed out, will be most helpful in verbalizing clearly many of the issues that are constantly being discussed in regards to priests from other countries coming to serve in the United States. Since the church is at the very center of the globalizing world community, and since our country comprises all the ethnic nationalities of the world living in common spaces and in the same period of time, new challenges will emerge and new pastoral responses will have to be devised. But we should not be afraid. We should have imagination, courage, and a creative spirit so that our church can meet the needs of our present age. We have nothing to fear except our own fears, for the Spirit will guide us through uncharted ways into new and ever more exciting possibilities.

Rev. Virgilio Elizondo has been a priest, scholar, and activist for forty-two years. He is a native of San Antonio, born of Mexican immigrants. In 1972 he founded the Mexican-American Cultural Center. At present he is director of Catholic Television of San Antonio and Distinguished Professor at the University of Notre Dame.

Appendix

Research Methods and Additional Data Tables

The Survey of Dioceses and Institutes

In order to know the numbers and locations of international priests, we decided to survey dioceses and religious institutes. In the questionnaire we asked about their policies, programs, and greatest problems concerning international priests. In March 2004 we sent a three-page questionnaire to all 193 dioceses and the 100 largest religious institutes. After making many reminder calls, we received 151 completions from dioceses and 58 from religious orders. Thus the response rate was 78 percent for the dioceses and 58 percent for the institutes—71 percent total.

The Survey of International Priests

In 2002 we experimented with asking dioceses and religious institutes to provide names and addresses of international priests in order to compile a complete list. The level of cooperation was very low, so we abandoned the idea. Instead, we tried to assemble a list by working through groups of international priests. We phoned all Aniedi Okure's contacts and asked for help. Some provided us lists. For example, the Korean priests possess an up-to-date directory, which they gave us. The Hispanic priests have a loose national organization whose address list they provided to us; since it did not include all Hispanic priests, we needed to supplement it with other lists.

We phoned diocesan vicars of priests, leaders of international priest groups, and friends, asking for help. After three months we had a list of approximately 1,000 international priests taken from 23 different sources, a list that was as representative as possible. We cannot claim that the list is a random sample.

A major difficulty is that we asked for the names of priests born overseas whose ministry in the United States began in 1985 or later. The persons providing us with lists lacked information on the place of birth and date of beginning ministry here, so they resorted to guessing. In the case of Hispanic priests, some on the lists turned out to have been born in the United States, not overseas. In a word, the information given us by our friends was inaccurate.

We aimed to study a sample that represented all nations in correct proportions. But this raised a further problem: nobody could tell us how many Koreans, Indians, or Hispanics should be in our sample of 1,000. The only data available to us was a survey done by CARA in 1999 (Froehle et al. 1999). It provided estimates of numbers from each nation, but not numbers of those who began ministry in 1985 or later. For example, the CARA list had a very large number from Ireland, but the vast majority came to the United States in the 1950s, 1960s, and 1970s.

After asking international priests for estimates from each nation, we used the best information available. The sample ended up totaling 1,019, and it is described in Table A.1 (p. 153).

Mailing was done in batches between May and July 2004, with two waves going to each priest. Of the 1,019 we sent, 35 were returned to us due to bad addresses, leaving 984 that went to good addresses. As of late September we received 227 questionnaires from priests who fit the criteria and 101 from priests who did not (three-fourths of whom had begun ministry here prior to 1985). Of the good 227 questionnaires, 170 were from diocesan priests and 57 were from religious.

Since only 227 of the 328 returns were eligible (.692), we could assume that a similar proportion of eligibles would be in the non-return list. Thus, .692 of the 984 sent out to good addresses gives us 681 eligible priests, and 227 is a 33 percent return. This is as good an estimate as we can make.

On the bottom of the last page of the questionnaire we asked, "Would you be willing to be interviewed by telephone about topics in this survey?" One hundred thirty priests said yes and gave us a phone number or e-mail address. Later we tried to phone a random sample of 40 of them, and we soon succeeded in interviewing 20.

We asked these 20 men why, in their judgment, the response rate was only 33 percent, since other recent surveys of priests attained response rates of at least 69 percent. They gave us several reasons. A major reason is that some of our lists were old, and in many rectories nobody forwards a letter or returns it to the sender if the priest no longer lives there. The secretary simply throws it into the wastebasket. This problem undoubtedly lowered our response rate and introduced a bias in that the priests in our survey are men who moved less often than average.

Another influence depressing the response rate was that many international priests have a distrust of questionnaires, and some are not confident about their written English. In addition, a certain number feel uncertainty about their status as priests, so they avoid expressing their attitudes and feelings openly, even in an anonymous survey. Taking account of all these clues, we conclude that our survey over-represents international priests who are less transient than average, who are accustomed to questionnaires, whose English is good, and who generally feel at home in the American church.

Interviews and Focus Groups

We talked with a hundred persons about the issues in our study, including 86 interviews and three focus groups that we recorded on tape. We asked officers of the National Federation of Priests' Councils to nominate vicars of priests, and we asked lay ministers and religious educators to nominate peers whom we should call. As noted earlier, we tried to reach 40 of the international priests who returned surveys. We phoned persons directing the best-known acculturation programs in the nation, and all of them gave us good interviews. In the end we taped interviews with 20 international priests, 8 American priests, 20 vicars and bishops, 28 lay leaders and laypersons, and 11 directors of acculturation programs. We carried out three focus groups in different locations.

Dean Hoge did most of the phone interviews, with assistance from Eugene Hemrick. Aniedi Okure led the focus groups. All were transcribed and entered into a computer using the NVivo program.

Table A.1
Population and Sample by Nation of Origin

	Estimated Population Percent	Number Sent	Number Received Who Fit	Percent of Sample
Latin America, including Brazil and Caribbean	19	290	50	22
Canada	1	0	0	0
Africa:				
Nigeria	6	)	22	10
		) 110		
All Other Africa	8	)	15	7
Asia:				
Philippines	10	103	24	11
India	11	109	40	18
Vietnam	12	120	26	12
All Other Asia	7	74	22	10
Europe:				
Italy	3	7	4	2
Ireland	2	10	2	1
Poland	8	80	12	5
Spain and Portugal	8	101	7	3
All Other Europe	5	15	3	1
Total	100	1019	227	102

Table A.2
Life History (in Percents)

		Diocesan	Religious
	Number of cases =	170	57
Present age	39 or younger	24	37
	40–49	44	33
	50–59	21	23
	60–69	9	5
	70 or older	2	2
	Mean Age	47	45

In what year did you come to the United States?

	Diocesan	Religious
1960–1969	1	4
1970–1979	4	5
1980–1989	18	23
1990–1999	42	35
2000 or later	34	33
Mean Year	1994	1993

How long do you expect to stay in the United States?

	Diocesan	Religious
For a year or less	5	4
2 or 3 years	13	7
4 or 5 years	9	13
More than 5 years	34	32
Uncertain	39	45

(if diocesan priest) Are you incardinated in the diocese?

	Diocesan
Yes	34
No	54
I intend to	12

(if religious priest) Are you affiliated with a religious institute in the United States?

	Religious
Yes	89
No	11

Table A.3
Training of International Priests (in Percents)

	Diocesan	Religious
In which country did you complete your seminary studies?		
Africa	16	12
India	18	12
Asia and Pacific except India	20	25
Latin America	19	4
Europe, including Rome	8	25
United States	19	23
In which country were you ordained?		
Africa	16	11
India	18	13
Asia and Pacific except India	19	21
Latin America	18	4
Europe, including Rome	8	21
United States	20	30
In what year were you ordained?		
Before 1970	7	7
1970–1979	14	18
1980–1989	37	12
1990–1999	36	46
2000 or later	6	18
Mean Year	1986	1989
Are you associated with any Catholic apostolic movements, for example, Focolare, the charismatic renewal, or the Neo-Catechumenate?		
Yes	21	14
(if yes) Which ones? (N = 34; 8)		
Charismatic Renewal	53	50
Focolare	15	0

(continued)

Neo-Catechumenate	6	0
Christian Family Movement;		
Marriage Encounter	6	13
Cursillos de Cristiandid	12	38
Other	9	0

Do you have an advanced degree other than the
B.D., S.T.B., M.Div., or M.A. in theology?

Yes	39	30

   (if yes) What is the field?

Social science	24	35
Natural science	3	6
Philosophy or theology (advanced)	46	35
Other	27	24

  In which country did you earn your
highest degree?

Africa	0	11
India	10	22
Asia and Pacific except India	5	11
Latin America	10	0
Europe, including Rome	34	17
United States	40	39

Are you a full-time student?

Yes	11	16

Table A.4
Coming to the United States (in Percents)

	Diocesan	Religious
What was your primary reason for coming to the United States?		
Studies	18	14
Ministry	61	61
Join family	4	9
Refugee	11	11
Other	5	5
When you began ministry in the United States, did you initiate it or was it initiated by your bishop or religious superior?		
My initiative	37	14
My Bishop/Religious Superior	43	70
Initiated by the U.S. church	19	11
Other	1	5
Do you have any family members living near your place of ministry?		
Yes	31	18
When you first arrived in the United States, did you have a formal welcome by other priests or by your place of ministry?		
Yes	64	60
When you first arrived in the United States, did you attend any program for orientation or acculturation?		
Yes	33	35
(if yes) Which one? (N = 56; 19)		
COPIP or COPIM in California	5	0
Oblate School of Theology, San Antonio	4	26

(continued)

Maryknoll Fathers	2	21
Program by one's own order or diocese	13	11
English language or accent reduction program (unspecified)	18	21
Cultural training (unspecified)	23	5
Other	36	16

How long did it last? (N = 53; 18)

Less than 2 weeks	49	33
1 to 6 months	25	33
8 to 12 months	19	6
More than 12 months	8	28

Was it helpful? Yes	96	100

(if it was helpful) What was helpful? (N = 47; 18)

Improved language skills or preaching skills	21	6
Improved cultural understanding, less culture shock	43	72
Better understanding of the local diocese or parish	32	22
Other	4	0

Did you have a formal mentor or formal support network during your first three years in the United States?

Yes	33	51

(if yes) Please describe it. (N = 47; 22)

Priests from my same country	9	5
Priests from my diocese, deanery, or congregation	21	46
The vicar for clergy; a spiritual director; the pastor; parish staff	51	36
Students or professors in the school	13	14
Other	6	0

(continued)

Are you now a naturalized citizen of the United States?

Yes	37	31
No	48	56
I intend to become	15	13

Did the diocese or religious community help you
with immigration processes?

Yes	62	72
No	30	17
Does not apply	8	11

Table A.5
Current Ministry (in Percents)

	Diocesan	Religious
Do you have an official assignment from the diocese or religious institute you work for?		
Yes	88	88
What is your primary ministry (not including being a student) in the United States?		
Pastor	19	25
Parochial Vicar	57	41
Teacher or Professor	1	2
Formation; Novice Master	2	4
Chaplain or Spiritual Director (of a specific group or ministry)	19	23
Part-time parish ministry; on call; "in residence"	2	2
Other	0	4
(if diocesan and not incardinated) Is there a letter of agreement between the bishop of your home diocese and the diocese in the United States where you are ministering?		
Yes	83	
No	13	
Don't know	4	
(if religious and not affiliated) Is there a letter of agreement between your home provincial and the diocese in the United States where you are ministering?		
Yes		83
No		11
Don't know		6

(continued)

(if not incardinated or affiliated) Are you
receiving a salary for your ministry here?

Yes	93	84

Do you regularly send money from your personal
income to help support your family in your
home country?

Yes	49	13

Since you began ministry in the U.S., have you
raised money from parishioners to support your
diocese, religious order, or mission project
in your home country?

Yes	19	11

Table A.6
Recommendations (in Percents)

	Diocesan	Religious
What would you recommend to assist the ministries of priests born in other countries, who are now living in the United States? (up to two ideas coded)		
Provide acculturation training, including English	50	52
Establish periodic gatherings and support groups	25	12
Assure equal treatment; no discrimination	21	15
Provide more support from the diocese	15	21
Provide clearer rules and guidance	15	18
Provide acceptance and spiritual support from Americans	11	15
Integrate specific ministry to diocese's work	1	3
Other	3	9
Should church leaders encourage priests to minister in cultures other than their own? If yes, why? If no, why not?		
Yes, it broadens priests'views and strengthens the universality of the church	73	68
Yes, to help with the priest shortage	5	11
Yes, to help the missionary work of the church	5	6
Yes, other	7	9
Yes (no explanation)	5	4
No, we should uphold the universal culture of the church, not local cultures	1	0
No, there is enough work to do in one's own culture	1	2
No (no explanation)	1	0

Table A.7
Policies of Dioceses and Institutes (in Percents)

	Dioceses	Religious Institutes
Do you have a policy for accepting priests from other countries for ministry?		
Yes	64	55
If yes, what is it?		
We follow USCCB guidelines, in total or in part.	69	3
We follow our own policy.	29	94
Other or uncodable.	3	3
Do you have a policy of incardinating or affiliating priests from other countries?		
Yes	59	36
If yes, what is it?		
We follow canon law guidelines on incardination (plus three years of service).	63	3
We follow guidelines for religious communities.	6	93
The priest must work in the diocese a minimum of five years.	19	3
The priest must serve in at least two parishes.	8	0
None are incardinated; they are accepted on a temporary basis only.	3	0

Table A.8
Dioceses and Institutes: Programs for Contact and Connections
(in Percents)

	Dioceses	Religious Institutes
How do you maintain contact with non-incardinated priests from other countries who reside within your diocese or province?		
Regular communications, similar to all other priests in the diocese	87	9
Communications and visitation, similar to all other priests in the diocese	1	79
Special visitation	6	12
Special orientation	6	0
Other	1	0
What policies or programs have facilitated closer connections between priests from other countries and priests born in the United States?		
Regular gatherings of priests, retreats, conferences, deanery meetings, and socials	85	19
Mentoring program or support program	12	68
Other	4	13

Table A.9
Dioceses and Institutes: Salaries, Health Plans,
Endorsements, and Mentors (in Percents)

	Dioceses	Religious Institutes
If a non-incardinated priest (not a student priest) from another country is in full-time pastoral ministry, do the following apply to him?		
Does this priest receive a salary?		
Yes	99	73
No	1	19
Don't know	0	8
Is the priest provided a health plan?		
Yes	97	90
No	3	5
Don't know	1	5
Is there a letter of agreement between the local diocesan bishops and the sending bishop or religious superior?		
Yes	92	79
No	6	13
Don't know	1	8
Is there financial provision for his training?		
Yes	61	80
No	32	15
Don't know	7	5
Is he included in the retirement plan?		
Yes	35	58
No	58	32
Don't know	7	11
Is a priest designated to be his mentor?		
Yes	37	54
No	60	36
Don't know	4	10

Table A.10
Dioceses and Institutes: Main Challenges (in Percents)

	Dioceses	Religious Institutes
What are the main challenges your diocese or religious institute has experienced in recent years with regard to priests born in other countries? (Open-ended; up to three ideas coded)		
Poor English language pronunciation; refusal to learn	70	31
Cultural insensitivity; cultural issues in either direction	60	33
Different ecclesiology, problems of accepting leadership of the laity	11	14
Treatment of women	15	0
Poor communication between American and foreign-born priests	8	3
Problems with immigration and INS	7	3
Problems of raising money for the home country	5	3
Difficulty of doing adequate background checks	6	0
Understanding diocesan policies, including annulment	5	0
Racism by Americans	3	3
Other	20	21

Table A.11
Dioceses and Institutes: Main Changes Desired (in Percents)

	Dioceses	Religious Institutes
What changes would you like to see in your diocese or religious institute to address the issues you have indicated? (open-ended; up to three ideas coded)		
More comprehensive orientation programs; more enculturation	48	24
Better language training	16	14
A program for sensitizing the native-born to cultural differences	5	7
Better mentoring by American priest	8	3
Solve problems on ecclesiology and minorities in America	3	7
Better screening process prior to acceptance	7	2
A program to foster relations with other priests	3	2
Better communication between dioceses and religious communities	1	5
Should train foreign-born seminarians here	3	2
Solve problems with immigration and INS	1	2
Other	23	16

References

"Africa's Health Care Brain Drain." 2004. *New York Times,* August 19. www.nytimes.com, accessed February 18, 2005.

Asmar, Marwan. 2003. "Stop the Brain Drain from the Arab World." Gulf News, December 29. Gulf News Research Centre Global News Wire. Al Nirs Publishing LLC. Accessed February 22, 2005, from Lexis-Nexis Academic database.

Bevans, Stephen B., and Roger P. Schroeder. 2004. *Constants in Context: A Theology of Mission for Today.* Maryknoll, NY: Orbis Books.

Camarota, Steven A., and Nora McArdle. 2003. "Where Immigrants Live: An Examination of State Residence of the Foreign Born by Country of Origin in 1990 and 2000." Center for Immigration Studies, www.cis .org/articles/2003/back1203, accessed January 28, 2005.

The CARA Report, Vol. 10, No. 4 (Spring 2005), "Graduate-Level Seminarians Increase Slightly in 2004–2005," p. 6.

Carrington, William J., and Enrica Detragiache. 1999. "How Extensive Is the Brain Drain?" *Finance and Development,* Vol. 36, No. 2, June [electronic version]. Washington, DC: International Monetary Fund. www.imf.org/external/pubs, accessed February 18, 2005.

Congregation for the Evangelization of Peoples. 2001. *Instruction on the Sending Abroad and Sojourn of Diocesan Priests from Mission Territories.* Vatican City, April 25.

Daly, William P. *The Laborer Is Worthy of His Hire: A Survey of Priests' Compensation in the Roman Catholic Dioceses of the United States. 2005* edition. Chicago, IL: National Federation of Priests' Councils, 2005.

Dolan, Jay P. 1985. *The American Catholic Experience.* Garden City, NY: Doubleday.

Dries, Angelyn. 1998. *The Missionary Movement in American Catholic History.* Maryknoll, NY: Orbis Books.

Ejime, Paul. 2005. "Arresting Brain Drain from Africa." Panafrican News Agency, Global News Wire–Asia Africa. November 24. Accessed February 22, 2005, from Lexis-Nexis Academic database.

Ellis, John Tracy. 1971. "The Formation of the American Priest: An Historical Perspective." In John Tracy Ellis, ed., *The Catholic Priest in the United States: Historical Investigations.* Collegeville, MN: Saint John's University Press. Pp. 3–110.

Fetterman, Mindy. 2005. "Pampered Pooches Nestle in Lap of Luxury." *U.S.A. Today,* February 11, pp. 1A, 2A.

Fix, Michael E., and Jeffrey S. Passel. 1994. "Immigration and Immigrants: Setting the Record Straight." Urban Institute. www.urban.org/urlprint .cfm?ID-5868, accessed January 28, 2005.

Froehle, Bryan T., Mary E. Bendyna, and Mary L. Gautier. 1999. *Priest Personnel Profile and Diocesan Pastoral Strategies.* Washington, DC: Center for Applied Research in the Apostolate, Georgetown University.

Gannon, Michael V. 1971. "Before and After Modernism: The Intellectual Isolation of the American Priest." In John Tracy Ellis, ed., *The Catholic Priest in the United States: Historical Investigations.* Collegeville, MN: Saint John's University Press. Pp. 293–383.

Glaser, William A. 1978. *The Brain Drain: Emigration and Return.* Oxford, UK: Pergamon Press.

Hennessy, James. 1981. *American Catholics.* New York: Oxford University Press, 1981.

Herbert, Ross, and Trish Guy. 2003. "Brain Drain in Africa Can Be Harnessed." *New Vision* (Uganda), October 27. Global News Wire–Asia Africa Intelligence. Accessed February 24, 2005, from Lexis-Nexis Academic database.

Hoge, Dean R. 1987. *The Future of Catholic Leadership: Responses to the Priest Shortage.* Kansas City, MO: Sheed & Ward.

Hoge, Dean R., Charles Zech, Patrick McNamara, and Michael J. Donahue. 1996. *Money Matters: Personal Giving in American Churches.* Louisville, KY: Westminster John Knox.

Hoge, Dean R., and Jacqueline E. Wenger. 2003. *Evolving Visions of the Priesthood.* Collegeville, MN: Liturgical Press.

Jasso, Guillermina, Douglas S. Massey, Mark R. Rosenzweig, and James P. Smith. 2003. "Exploring the Religious Preferences of Recent Immigrants to the United States." Ch. 12 in Yvonne Y. Haddad, Jane I. Smith, and John L. Esposito, eds. *Religion and Immigration.* New York: Altamira Press. Pp. 217–53.

Kemper, John C., S.S. "A Language of Caring." *The Priest,* April 1999, pp. 38–42.

Morris, Charles R. 1997. *American Catholic.* New York: Random House.

Perko, F. Michael. 1989. *Catholic and American: A Popular History.* Huntington, IN: Our Sunday Visitor Press.

Rai, Saritha. 2004. "Short on Priests, U.S. Catholics Outsource Prayers to Indian Clergy." *New York Times,* June 13. www.query.nytimes.com, accessed March 10, 2005.

Smith, William L. 2000. "Contemporary Irish Priests in America." In Joanne M. Greer and David O. Moberg, eds., *Research in the Social Scientific Study of Religion,* Vol. 11. Stamford, CT: JAI Press. Pp. 193–207.

_____. 2004. *Irish Priests in the United States: A Vanishing Subculture.* Dallas, TX: University Press of America.

Stalker, Peter. 2001. *The No-Nonsense Guide to International Migration.* Oxford, UK: New Internationalist/Verso.

Vegh, Steven G. 2004. "Foreign Priests Fill Persistent Vacancies in the U.S. Dioceses; Dozens Have Come to Va. From Abroad." *The Virginian Pilot and The Ledger-Star,* January 4, p. A1.

Index